FACILITATING LIVE ONLINE LEARNING

COLIN STEED

© Copyright 2011 Colin Steed

First published in 2011.

ISBN: 978-0-9569431-0-1

Copyright acknowledgement

 Published by Engaged Online Learning Ltd

Contents

Preface

The learning and development landscape is changing. Budgets for L&D are being cut whilst, at the same time, employers are demanding that more employees be trained. Learning professionals, with fewer resources at their disposal, are now exploring new workplace performance online tools for ways of delivering learning to more people.

In today's economic climate, with many organisations looking for ways to further reduce expenditure, a trend being observed throughout the world is that many L&D departments are losing classroom space to save on property costs. But it is important to remember that cost savings are not the primary reason for adopting live online learning. As you will discover in the following chapters, live online learning can often provide better and more effective learning experiences for our learners.

Our learners' needs are changing too. Today's learners want to learn in shorter timescales, they want learning accessible at the point of need, they want shorter sessions, and they want those sessions focused on the role they perform in the workplace.

With the majority of people now able to access Internet-enabled computers both at work and at home—even in their briefcase or in their pocket—the age of the virtual classroom has finally arrived.

Live online learning is not new – it has been around since the 1990s

Contrary to popular opinion, however, live online training—also called virtual classroom training or synchronous training—is not new. My first experience with it was back in 1995, when I was editor of *IT Training* magazine and was invited to try out a new technology which "would see the end of the classroom". How many times have we heard that old phrase every time something new is launched?

I was introduced to Centra, then probably the leading web conferencing system. This really sparked my enthusiasm for the subject and all the possibilities it could bring to the world of education and training, and I wrote one of the first books on the subject in 1998 called *Web Based Training*.

The ability to train whenever and wherever the learners were had tremendous appeal—but despite the hype and the tremendous marketing put behind this revolutionary method, it was largely ignored by organisations. Some of the corporate giants did invest in the systems, which were generally hosted by the organisations themselves, but on the whole it became lost in the mixing pot that was corporate training in the 1990s.

At the time, I remember interviewing many corporate trainers in order to discover their views on this new way of bringing learning into their organisations. Not surprisingly perhaps, they were on the whole sceptical at best and completely disparaging at worst. In general, the view was that, no matter what benefits the technology could offer, it could never produce the quality of learning that could be accomplished by trainers in the face-to-face classroom.

Few believed it possible to recreate the same 'feel' of the face-to-face experience. They thought it would be impossible to observe learners' problems and offer solutions. They thought they would miss the subtle cues of body language, and would be unable to tell whether the learners were actually learning anything. All fair points, it must be said.

- Although I was excited by the possibilities and opportunities that live online training could bring to our organisations, I did have some major concerns as to its likely success. Firstly, my main concern was the fledgling technology; not only was the software new, but organisations were in the very early days of using the Internet. Would it be up to the job, or was it a step too far? Additionally, would the trainers brought up on the classroom buy into this new method of delivery? Following the interviews I had conducted with trainers from some of those early adopting organisations, I had severe doubts. And finally, would organisations realise that the trainers would need to acquire a new set of additional—but complementary—skills? Or would they just repeat their classroom sessions online?

- However, as I said, some of the organisations with large training budgets did bite the bullet and did spend large amounts of money in purchasing a system. These early adopters had mixed success.

- Many training managers dismissed the online tools as unusable or impractical due to the high costs of licensing, the learning curve for trainers and users, and problems caused by lack of the necessary Internet bandwidth. Even those organisations that hosted the systems internally had frequent connection and bandwidth problems. Users and trainers would need dedicated technical support, too. The managers decided the tools weren't worth the cost and the effort required.

- The users were not particularly enamoured with it either. The so-called 'learning experience' that they were promised with live online learning turned out to be nothing more than pure lectures, often for hours on end, as the trainers were trying to replicate the classroom environment online. The learners found the sessions boring and slow; lack of eye contact, endless PowerPoint slides, and hectic schedules ensured that learners would soon switch off.

- I have no doubt that for some organisations those early days of web-based training—as it was then called—were successful. But it is safe to say that the use and reputation of live online learning quickly faded into the distance as a viable method of delivering learning experiences.

So what has changed?

During the past decade or so, powered by the huge and rapid advances in technology and years of research into how people learn online, things have developed and progressed considerably. Notably, the following advances have been made which has brought reliable live online learning to everyone:

- Most people now enjoy a fast Internet connection through high-speed Broadband both at work and at home, indeed even while they are travelling, by the advances in mobile technology such as smart phones and internet-enabled tablets, such as the iPad.

- Nearly everyone has computer access at work and at home, as well as owning many Internet-enabled mobile wireless devices capable of receiving learning events.

- The web conferencing software has evolved into a reliable platform, benefitting from over 10 years of development and enhancement.

- We have been provided with evidence-based research on how people learn online and the best way to deliver online learning events.

- The recession has necessitated every organisation carrying out deep cost-cutting exercises; organisations both public and private are looking for all ways to save on non-essential costs.

And so it is, within this climate, that we have seen a dramatic rise and re-emergence of live online learning throughout the world. This time around, however, we do have a much better chance of reaping those benefits and opportunities—but only if we act on the lessons we have learnt from the past.

Lessons Learned

So what lessons have we learnt since the 1990s?

- Firstly, and most importantly, we understand that the face-to-face classroom trainer cannot simply transfer their classroom delivery skills or their content into the online classroom. As you will discover, although much of the trainer's skills can be utilised online, there are many new skills and techniques needed to ensure delivery of effective, learner-focused and engaging online events.

- Next, we now understand that web conferencing systems themselves will not automatically provide good learning experiences, in much the same way as using PowerPoint will not automatically create great slide presentations. In an effective online classroom event, the technology is there simply to provide the facilities that trainers need to be able to deliver the learning—and it should remain transparent to the learners. In other words, the technology should be in the background providing the tools for the trainer to facilitate learning.

- Thirdly, we have some evidence–based research, on how we learn online, from educational psychologists like Sweller, Mayer, Clark, and Medina. These findings prove that to enable learners to learn in the online environment we need to overhaul the traditional way trainers produce visual aids, and we must understand how not to overload our learners' working memories if we want the learning to stick.

- An important new lesson we have learnt is that we need to produce shorter, learner-centred events that are focused on enabling learners to learn and practise skills that are aligned to what they need to do in their job. We need to stop dumping information into our learners—and that means a complete re-think of how we design our online events.

- Trainers need to think beyond the physical aspects of classroom and instead create learning relationships with their learners, using the resources available to them in the online classroom. These learning relationships require the trainer to master new facilitation skills and techniques, as well as acquire mastery of different tools and resources from the ones deployed when the trainer and learners are in the same room together.

We will be covering all these topics and more throughout the book.

Who is this book for?

This book is for trainers and all those who will be facilitating live online learning events. Whether you are a complete novice to the subject or have presented many live online sessions, you will find many useful techniques, tips and best practice guidelines for planning, designing and facilitating live online sessions that are interactive, participative and collaborative, and that achieve improved performance both for your learners and their organisations.

The types of live online learning events that you will be able to deliver successfully include courses, sales presentations, product demonstrations, company briefings, product launches—in fact the list of event types is virtually endless.

What is this book about?

In this book we focus solely on facilitating small group online learning events. We do not cover the techniques of running webinars or live online meetings, although many of the skills you will learn are just as relevant to these too.

An important point to understand is that the book does not cover the technicalities of using web conferencing systems. You will certainly need to learn the specific techniques of using the particular web conferencing system you will be using. I do recommend, however, that you actually learn how to do that online—not in a classroom.

In the book I have provided screenshots of one of the leading web conferencing systems, WebEx Training Centre. However, you will be able to apply the skills and techniques we will be covering in the book to any of the leading web conferencing systems.

Let's have a look at each chapter and what we are going to cover in each.

Chapter 1: Introducing the Live Online Classroom

The re-emergence of the virtual classroom; the benefits and challenges; comparing the virtual classroom with other instructional methods; web conferencing systems; how could your organisation use web conferencing?; can anything be taught in the virtual classroom?

Chapter 2: Role and skills of the Online Learning Facilitator

Differences between classroom and online skills; what skills are required?; what does the live online trainer do?; carrying out the live online trainer's role; equipment and facilities you need

Chapter 3: Designing your content

How do we learn?; cognitive load theory; learner-centred events; guided discovery; action mapping; objectives or outcomes?

Chapter 4: Designing your slides

Why are slides so poor?; cognitive load and visuals; graphic design fundamentals; assertion/evidence model; visualising your message; choosing your visuals – photographs, charts and diagrams, animation; text and type; using colour

Chapter 5: Preparing your session

Knowing your learners; preparing your learner and facilitator guides; preparing a session plan; preparing your content; setting up your online classroom; rehearsing; using a co-facilitator/host; preparing your learners

Chapter 6: Communicating in the online classroom

Using your voice effectively; posing questions; gauging learner participation; communicating using online classroom response facilities

Chapter 7: Managing your session

How to open your session; handling latecomers; when technology fails; dealing with questions; sharing applications; sharing your web browser;

sharing web content; using breakout rooms; managing discussions; managing group work

Chapter 8: Maximising learner engagement

Rules of engagement; making it learner-centred; questioning for engagement; using icebreakers; handling Q&As; some do's and don'ts

Chapter 9: Closing your session and following up

Closing your session; assessing your learners' achievements; assessing your own performance; following up with your learners to continue the learning

Acknowledgements

It is only possible to write a book with the help, guidance and counselling of others and this book is an excellent example of this.

Over the past eleven years, I have had the pleasure of serving the Institute's many thousands of individual and corporate members, and they have been a valued help to me in the early stages when I was planning the content of the book.

Additionally, I would like to thank the Institute Board—notably Donald Taylor, Edmund Monk and Colin Thompson, who gave me their encouragement to write the book.

Additionally, I am indebted to my lead tutors of the Certified Online Learning Facilitator course, Michelle Parish and Stuart Box, who have given me so much, in terms of help, advice and many hours of assistance in the development of the certification programme and the compilation of the standards that we work to.

I would also like to thank Sylvia Fielding, of CommaSense, who has extensively improved the book in terms of readability and clarity, Sheena

Whyatt for all her help with formatting the book, and Peter Labrow for the cover design.

I also want to thank the following authors whose books have been an inspiration to me: Ruth Colvin Clark & Ann Kwinn, Cindy Huggett, Jennifer Hoffman, Garr Reynolds, Cliff Atkinson, Nancy Duarte, Carmine Gallo, and Karen Hyder.

But most of all, I want to acknowledge and thank Jonathan Kettleborough for the many hours of discussions we had about the content, as well as for the expert advice and guidance he provided. His excellent critiques and frequent challenges to my assertions and views have made a real difference to the book.

Researching and writing this book has been a real labour of love for me— I hope that you gain as much from it as I have from writing it. I wish you good luck with facilitating live online learning events and I hope that it brings you a rewarding career and your learners a valuable learning experience.

We should all try to learn something every day. I have learnt just how valuable and important my friends and colleagues are.

Colin Steed
June 2011

1

Introducing the Online Classroom

Live instructor-led online learning—sometimes called synchronous or virtual classroom learning—has ushered in a new age in distance learning.

The attraction for organisations to be able to offer more training for less—through travel and accommodation cost savings, combined with the rapid deployment of training to large numbers of learners—has led to a sharp increase in the use of live online learning in recent years, both in the US and Europe.

In a survey conducted in the US by the American Society of Training and Development (2009), live online learning in the corporate sector has risen dramatically in the last few years—from 10% in 2003 to over 27% in 2009.

In the UK and Europe, we have witnessed similar percentage increases. Latest predictions are that live online learning will make dramatic changes to the way learning is delivered in the future, with 46% of UK organisations stating that they intend utilising live online learning this year (Towards Maturity Benchmark 2011).

These figures were confirmed by the IITT Learning Survey (2011), which showed that 44% of UK organisations anticipated making increased use of live online learning in the future.

Another survey, published by the e-Learning Guild (2010), revealed that live online learning was used by 66% of the 3,327 US organisation members who responded to the survey. According to the report's author Patti Shank, almost all of the respondents agreed or strongly agreed that online tools and the opportunities they provide were "essential to their organisation".

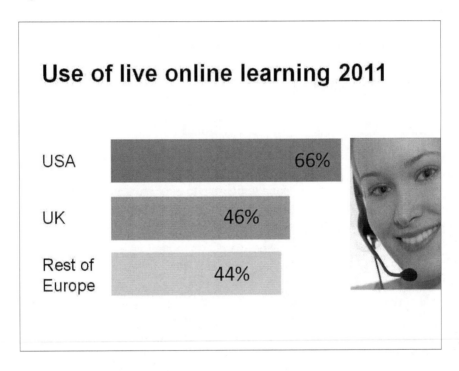

Use of live online learning 2011

USA	66%
UK	46%
Rest of Europe	44%

The use of live online learning is expanding rapidly throughout the world

All of these recent studies show that there is, without doubt, a significant and rapidly growing take-up of live online learning throughout the world.

The recent economic climate has also made a significant impact on the situation. In the ASTD (2009) survey, the authors stated that some 70% of organisations were "actively looking at ways to become more cost efficient at delivering learning to their employees" and more than half had "restructured their learning from the classroom to virtual delivery". In the UK, the need to "reduce the time away from the job" was cited by 45% of organisations as a key driver (Towards Maturity Benchmark 2011). Additionally, 41% said that they "needed to reduce training delivery costs" and 35% said that they "needed to deliver learning in greater volume demanded by the business".

The survey respondents also indicated that they were "looking for new and less expensive ways to deliver learning like virtual learning solutions" and that they had "put restrictions on travel for learners".

The benefits and challenges of online learning

There is no doubt that live online learning is now making a significant impact on the learning delivery mix both in organisations and the educational sectors throughout the world but, as with all things 'e', this doesn't mean that "one size fits all."

I remember when the videodisc (or laserdisc) was launched back in the 1980s. It was announced with much media hype, with the result that some of the large employers quickly took up the challenge and began replacing classroom courses with video-based courses. At the time I was editor of *IT Training* magazine and was told that videodiscs would enable employees to learn by themselves and would provide employers with the opportunity to reduce the number of classroom-based courses.

Additionally, the pundits were having a field day, proclaiming that "it was the end of classroom training" and that it "would drastically cut the number of classroom trainers that were employed".

To some extent, the same was true with the launch of Computer-Based Training (CBT). It was claimed that CBT would mean the end of the classroom and trainers, as staff could learn on their own at their computers whenever and wherever they wanted. It would revolutionise how we learned, and employers would save on classroom and associated costs.

Although both of those delivery methods were a comparative success, they just didn't replace the classroom, despite many thinking they would. The majority of formal learning is still undertaken in the classroom, and trainers are still delivering courses.

However, recent studies from the IITT Learning Survey (2011) show that the learning delivery mix is changing to encompass a whole range of de-livery methods and the results of the current research studies show that live online learning is starting to make significant inroads as a significant player in formal training delivery.

But we have learnt some valuable lessons over the years.

- In the early years of technology-based learning, we had little in the way of qualitative research into how people learned using technology-delivered learning.

- The content designers were pioneers and were comparatively in-experienced in developing technology-delivered content that en-abled true learning to take place—the tools were not available and our knowledge of content creation for this medium was fairly basic and untested.

- It has taken many years of innovation and development to get to where we are today, with some excellent learner-centred e-learning projects in many global organisations. The days of those green/blue screens full of text and those page turners controlled by 'Click Next to Continue' buttons are definitely a thing of the past.

So as we embark on another new journey with live online learning, we must be mindful that we are still at the entry point and there are, without doubt, some huge challenges ahead that we will have to overcome. Let's explore them now.

We have been passed the baton from those e-learning pioneers and our challenge is to pick up the baton and run with what we have learnt from them. I hope this book will provide some valuable insights and lessons that will allow us to take advantage of the promises and opportunities that live online learning offers.

Let's now take a look at some of the benefits and challenges that live online learning can provide.

Benefits of live online learning

So what are the benefits of live online learning both for employers and learners?

The benefits to the organisation are many:

- reduced travel time and accommodation costs
- staff spend less time away from the job
- faster deployment of knowledge and skills
- higher completion rates compared to offline self-study
- opportunity to provide training to larger numbers of workers – at a much lower cost
- measurable
- trackable
- recordable
- easy to link with other learning
- minimum use of additional technology
- minimal capital outlays - no need to 'own' the technology

From a learning perspective, users cite the following benefits:

- shorter and more focused courses

- courses that are more interactive and collaborative

- greater opportunity to practise either in groups or individually

- ability to share with other learners

- ability to learn without having to leave the place of work

- ability to learn at a convenient time

- more likelihood of receiving 'Just in Time' learning

- probability of being trained more often and in a more timely way

Challenges of live online learning

But the live online learning environment is not problem-free. In addition to challenges with the technology—primarily due to the quality of the internet connection—users often report that many sessions lack interaction and engagement with the learners due to:

- poor facilitation skills of trainers/presenters

- desktop distractions/multi-tasking

- poor visual aid skills of trainers/presenters

- lack of understanding of live online content design

- management not seeing the benefits—apart from cost savings

- IT not providing the required support in some organisations, usually due to perceived security issues

But by far the biggest issue is the live online facilitator's lack of the requisite skills in the live online environment. It is the biggest hurdle that we face today if live online learning is to provide us with the promise and opportunities that are there for the taking. So why is this?

Employers—and many trainers—seem to be under the impression that their training staff can simply take their classroom courses and deliver them in the in the online classroom. This is a misguided and totally incorrect assumption. To be able to deliver quality learning events in the live online learning environment, trainers need a complete new layer of skills and techniques which they must overlay on their classroom design and delivery skills. They will definitely need to acquire these skills and techniques, and practise and hone them well, before their first live online session.

It is a huge challenge to get this point of view across to employers and, to some extent, the trainers themselves. Unfortunately, many trainers are either not convinced that they need new skills, or they do not believe that the medium is able to offer the same learning effectiveness as their trusty classrooms.

If we can create engaging learner-centred online events which eliminate distractions and change the way we present visual aids to aid learning—and, most importantly get the trainer/facilitator skills right—then we really do have the means to deliver on the huge potential that live online learning offers. In so doing we can greatly improve the performance and effectiveness of our organisations.

Does remote teaching hinder learning?

According to the many trainers I regularly talk to, some remain sceptical about the effectiveness of learning at a distance (that is, outside the physical confines of the classroom). They believe that the learner can only learn best when their trainer and fellow learners are in the same room.

The main concern of established trainers is that it is impossible to train a class if they are unable to physically see the all-important body language cues. It is a valid view, and it remains one of the most important challenges that live online trainers face. But it can be overcome as we shall see in this book.

Another often-quoted observation from classroom trainers is that, not being physically present under the watchful eye of the trainer, remote learners will be easily distracted, focusing on the ubiquitous emails, Twitter and instant messenger messages that appear on their computers at frequent intervals. "How can we expect them to concentrate on us when all of this is going on?" they say. Again, this is a valid point.

So does remote teaching actually hinder the learning process? The honest answer is yes, it can, and frequently does. Let me give you an example. I am sure that you, like me, have attended one of the many free webinars that are available and have started out full of interest. But soon, after the presenter has been droning on and on, reading out each bullet point on his slides, your mind starts to drift off to an important task that you need to complete before going home, or an email pings and shows up on your screen. The presenter is still droning on and on, so you immediately open the email message and start replying, with one ear on the presenter.

Been there, done that? Me too, often!

What I just described is typical of the type of live online session where the presenter did not possess the necessary skills to engage his audience. In our example, the 'presenter' was in full-on lecture mode, the visuals were not impactful (as a long list of bullet points they may as well have been a document), and the presenter made no effort to engage or involve the audience. Additionally, with those 'distractors' running on your computer, your involvement was immediately taken away from the presentation. So is it hardly surprising that this particular event hindered learning?

I can tell you that a trainer, correctly trained in how to produce engaging content and facilitate engaging learner-centred events, would not be running a session like the one described above.

Ensuring learning is effective

To take full advantage of the many opportunities offered by the live online learning environment, our new breed of online facilitators must learn a suite of new skills and techniques which complement their existing classroom skills. They will then be able to sense these all-important "body language cues", and will know how to help and encourage learners thereby creating engaging learning experiences.

Of course, like every training modality that has come before—classroom, CBT, e-learning, correspondence courses, video, and so on—there is no guarantee that the online training session will automatically translate into learning. The key to effective online learning is held by two groups of individuals: the instructional designer, and the trainer or facilitator. In reality, these two functions are frequently carried out by the same person.

Effective learning needs a base of solid instructional design, but if you have ever experienced a session run by a good classroom trainer, you know that what they do is way beyond what has been designed for the course. A trainer can bring real-life experience, humour and adaptability to a session, and create a comfortable engaging learning experience for the learners. We must strive to bring that to the online classroom too.

In the online classroom, it can be a challenge to capture that same level of connectedness that comes naturally in the classroom.

However, we must remember that this exciting new medium is just that; it is a medium. In other words, the web conferencing software does not guarantee effective learning. The software is simply the technology that provides the functions and facilities to allow a trainer or facilitator to use their skills and techniques to enable learners to learn in an effective manner. This is an important message for all employers!

Comparison with the instructional methods

Let's now explore the main instructional methods that we use today and compare them with the opportunities provided by the online classroom.

Taking each one, starting with face-to-face learning, we'll explore their plus and minus points.

Face-to-face classroom

Traditional classrooms are characterised by the trainer and the learners being in the same room, at the same time, and all involved in the same activities together. The trainer uses common tools such as a projector, whiteboards and flip charts, to assist in delivering content. Additionally, the use of breakout (or syndicate) rooms facilitates additional discussion and collaboration.

Of course, the advantages of the traditional classroom are many. The most important of these is that everyone is in a recognisable learning environment. Everyone is used to classrooms from nursery school through to university and on to the workplace. Trainers don't need to explain to the learners how they should interact, behave and learn. Learners can ask questions spontaneously, a sense of community can be developed, and they often appreciate being able to leave their regular place of work—sometimes away from their workplace—and learn in a new setting.

The trainer also knows how to manage this environment, especially as he has been trained that way too. Eye contact and body language are the all-important indicators to the trainer and help him direct pace and communication.

This method of instruction, however, does have its drawbacks.

- Classrooms are expensive in terms of the cost of accommodation, the expense of getting learners to the location, and the opportunity costs of the learners being away from their job, usually for extensive periods of time.

- Classrooms can only accommodate a certain number of learners—for a large workforce, many events will need to be run to accommodate all of the people being trained.

- The trainer can often try to be the star of the show with his method of presentation, jokes and demonstration of superior knowledge and skill.

- The cost of facilities can also be prohibitive, so every classroom has an associated property, maintenance, equipment and insurance cost.

Self-study

Self-study, or self-paced training, enables learners to learn at their own pace through books, CDs, videos, web-based tutorials (e-learning) and podcasts.

Learning through self-study has the major advantages that learners can learn at their own pace, at a time that is convenient to them, often out of working hours. I particularly make a lot of use of this form of learning.

On a fairly regular basis, using my iPad, I log into a web learning portal site where there is a huge range of self-study online tutorials on most of the major software applications. For a modest monthly fee, I can access learning whenever and wherever I can access the Internet. I find it a great way of learning, but it may not be for everyone.

However, self-study learning does have some drawbacks.

- Learners can find it difficult to motivate themselves to complete programmes due to lack of specific deadlines, deliverables and encouragement.
- It's a very passive medium and, although suited to some learning styles, it is best in short bursts; one to two hours is ideal.

Blended learning

Blended learning refers to a combination, or blend, of a number of different learning methods. Blended learning is becoming increasingly common as both organisations and learning designers realise the benefit of using appropriate media within the learning mix.

An example of a blended learning programme would be a course that consists of a traditional classroom session followed up by, say, a self-study session then, later, with a live online session. Throughout the event, social networks can be utilised to encourage the learners to collaborate using networking sites/forums and live chats.

Note that 'blended learning' does not necessarily imply only 'formal' learning such as courses, whether classroom, online, or e-learning. It can incorporate informal learning too; so a blended learning programme could comprise elements such as assignments, social learning, reading, practising on the job, and so on.

It is becoming apparent to many learning practitioners that the blended formats are the best way of accommodating different learning styles and supporting learning objectives where there are different types of learning required; for example, problem-solving skills, interpersonal skills, and skill-based learning. Consequently, today's trainers will often need to manage a combination of traditional, self-study, and online classroom training technologies.

Live online learning

Live online classroom instruction is led by a facilitator in real time over the Internet. The online classroom is characterised by group interaction and collaboration amongst learners under the guidance of a facilitator or trainer. It is essentially focused on the learner, not the instructor.

Discussion and problem-solving can be managed using a variety of tools and methods, and people in different cultures and personal situations can be involved at the same time from a variety of locations.

Of course, there are drawbacks, some of which we have already discussed; among these are:

- Problems encountered with online classroom instruction often start with the technology itself. If connection (or log-in) problems occur, or there is a poor audio connection, learners can often begin the experience with a negative impression.

- Some learners, and trainers who are currently classroom trainers, have difficulty believing that the online classroom can be as effective as the traditional classroom, and so do not fully commit to active participation.

But, as we shall see later, the main problem with live online classroom instruction is the classroom-based trainers themselves who believe they can use the techniques they have employed for many years in a live online classroom.

As you will see throughout this book, this is a totally incorrect and misguided assumption, as there are many new skills and techniques that the trainer must learn in order to conduct a successful online classroom event. That said, much of the trainer's knowledge of delivery, learning styles, questioning techniques, conducting discussions, adult learning theory, learner management, and so on is just as important and transferable to the online classroom environment.

Web Conferencing Systems

Let's now turn our attention to the software systems that provide the facilities for us to conduct live online learning events—we will refer to these as Web Conferencing Systems. Various vendors are now offering first-class products and services to enable us to run live online sessions. According to the e-Learning Guild Report 'Getting Started with Synchronous e-Learning' (2010), the top six web conferencing systems in use are:

- WebEx Training Centre (34.5%)

- Adobe Connect (27.6%)

- Microsoft Live Meeting (22.0%)

- Citrix GoToMeeting (13.8%)

- Elluminate Live! (now Blackboard Collaborate) (8.5%)

- Saba Centra (6.2%)

Selecting a web conferencing system is something that you should not go into lightly as there are various elements you will need to consider. Besides deciding whether to host the system or have it hosted by the vendor, you will need to decide what tools and facilities you will need. Although most include the basic facilities, certain systems do not have breakout rooms or whiteboards which, in my opinion, are vital for learning events.

Additionally, it is crucial that you get your IT department on your side, as they will be an important player in determining the success of your live online events. So if you are intending to select a system, make sure that you establish a good relationship with the IT department early and involve them in discussing the requirements for your events.

Assuming that you have a web conferencing system in place, let's look at the types of events you can run on it. There are three main types of events that web conferencing systems can deliver: Web Meetings, Webinars, and Learning Events. Let's take a look at each one to see what they are best used for and what their main differences are.

Web meetings

Web meetings are the online version of the face-to-face meeting. In web meetings, the software is used for small groups to meet online to collaborate, share documents and make decisions, wherever the participants are.

Common uses for web meetings include trainer meetings, sales meetings, management meetings and so on, but the software has uses elsewhere; notably for system/software support, coaching, and mentoring.

Webinars

Webinars are events where you want to distribute information or raise awareness to a large audience. A webinar is an online seminar, delivered by a presenter to an audience which may consist of many hundreds of people. At webinars, the presenter conducts a presentation and invites questions from the audience. These events are primarily presenter-focused, inasmuch as the presenter is the main focus for the event, as opposed to an online classroom event which is learner-centred. Webinars are very popular with organisations, allowing them to disseminate information to many learners at once. They are, however, quite passive for the learner, unless of course the presenter has the necessary skills to engage learners through frequent interaction.

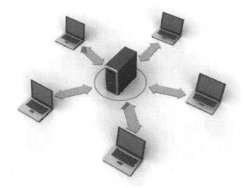

Learning events

Learning events are sessions with a small audience for providing performance-based outcomes.

They are live facilitator–led events which use the web conferencing system to provide the facilities for live online learning sessions.

This type of event is explicitly learner-centred as opposed to the 'broadcast' approach of webinars.

The skills and techniques required to run an effective learning event are the primary focus of this book, but many of these skills are also applicable for running meetings and webinars.

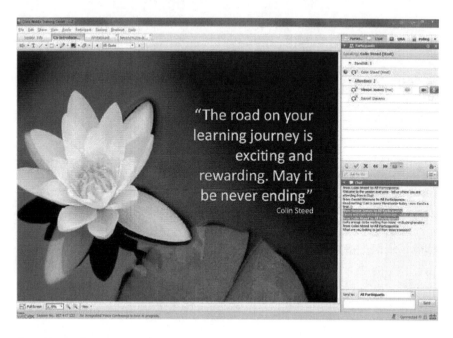

The Webex Training Centre user interface

Web conferencing: features and facilities

We have looked at the types of event that web conferencing systems can be used for.

Let's now have a brief look at the main features and facilities provided by typical web conferencing systems to enable you to deliver your online events. Note that I will just provide an overview here as we'll be looking in detail in later chapters at how to use them to best effect.

Audio

The audio facility enables the facilitator's voice to be heard and enables the facilitator and learners to talk to one another. Audio is delivered either via the Internet—Voice Over Internet Protocol (VOIP)—or by using a telephone connection. For an event to be successful, the quality of your audio signal is vital, so pay careful attention to getting the quality right. This means acquiring a fast reliable Internet connection and using a quality headset or microphone—more on this later.

Chat

Text-based chat allows the learners and facilitator to communicate with one another through text messaging. Private messaging enables learners to signal difficulties to the facilitator without disrupting the session. Often the facilitator will use Chat to ask learners to respond to questions. At first, learners are more likely to interact with Chat than by using a microphone, especially those who are shy. As a facilitator, you should constantly monitor the text Chat panel for any learner questions, as this will provide you with valuable feedback. Provided the facilitator gives permission, learners may also chat with other learners, either all at once or directly with another learner.

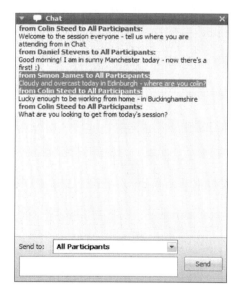

Emoticons/response icons

A useful way of obtaining feedback from your learners is to get them to use emoticons and response icons. These emoticons (for WebEx) are,

Raise Hand, Agree, Disagree, Slow Down, Speed Up, and a panel of Emoticons (you can see the Smiley Face here).

Other web conferencing systems may use other emoticons, but the principle remains the same. Encouraging your learners to use this form of feedback helps to make up for that 'loss of eye contact', so set an example by using them yourself on a frequent basis.

Polling

Another useful way of obtaining feedback is through the use of the polling feature (an online survey). One of the benefits of using the polling facility is that it allows for all learners to be active at the same time and provides real-time collated feedback from a large group of people.

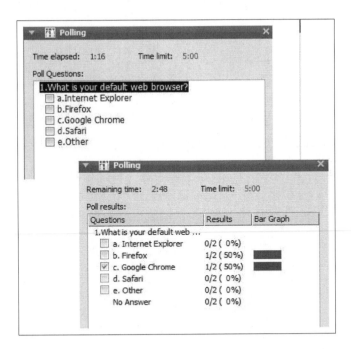

Polls are excellent for getting quick snapshots from the group

Polls are generally very easy to set up and they can help you get a quick check on the pulse of the class. For example, you could use a poll to get feedback on, say, the experience levels of your learners.

Remember to share the results with the class to foster a sense of community. However, if the results or are of a sensitive, personal or perhaps a security issue, it is best not to display them.

So just use the results to start a group discussion.

Whiteboard

The whiteboard facility is the online equivalent of a classroom whiteboard. The whiteboard has annotation (mark-up) tools which allow learners to add text, draw pictures and highlight items using the marker pen tool.

Whiteboards allow trainers and learners to post ideas, either by entering text or drawing, and it is a good way of getting learners working at the same time and engaged with the lesson.

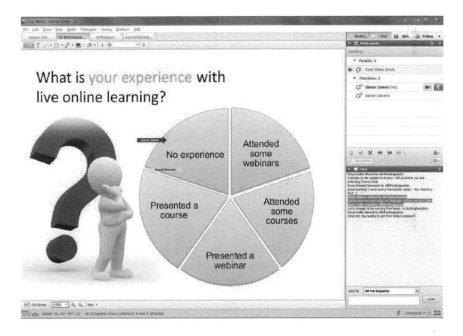

The annotation toolbar

One good use of the whiteboard is to ask learners at the start of the lesson to type in their expectations for the session and revisit them at the end. Try to promote discussions by asking learners to elaborate on their whiteboard input—your questioning skills need to come into play here.

Document share

Sharing documents is the most used facility in the online classroom. You display your slides by sharing your slide deck in the main viewer window to enable everyone to follow your presentation. You simply upload your slides and then click through as you would in the classroom by using your mouse, space bar or pointer. You can share other documents too: most systems can handle Microsoft Office documents, PDFs and various media files.

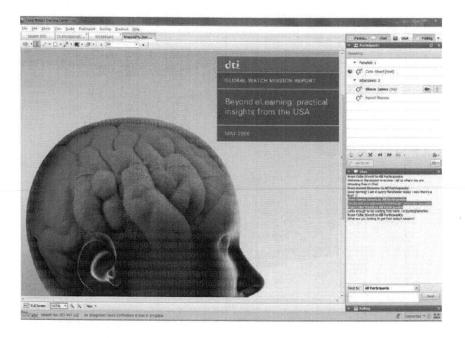

You obviously need to check what types of files the system you are look-ing at selecting can handle. Some systems will also allow you to enable your learners to download documents that you have uploaded. This is a really useful facility for, say, course materials you want to hand out, as well as the session slides—although if you follow my advice on slide de-sign, in Chapter 4, they won't be of much use!

Live video

Webcams using one- or two-way video streaming are provided by nearly all the main web conferencing systems. Being able to see the facilitator live (as well as the other learners) is a real bonus as it aids engagement and allows the facilitator to see the learner's body language in real time.

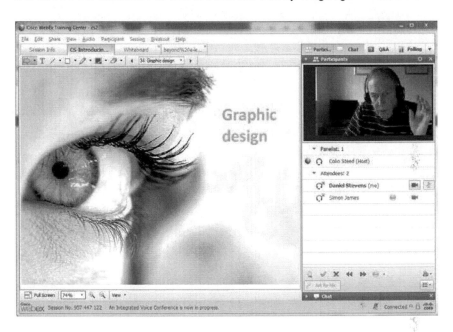

Using your webcam has many benefits – but be careful of over use

It does, however, have some drawbacks to consider. Live video is a very bandwidth-intensive feature which often limits its use to learners with very fast broadband connections but, even then, it can slow the system down. Video is excellent for your session opening, and perhaps for the Q&A

sessions, but my advice is not to use live video throughout the session, as it can be very distracting for the learners—you want them to be concentrating on your slides and not you—and it can create bandwidth issues.

Application sharing

This feature allows you to share software applications running on your computer with the learners. There are many variations of this feature, ranging from 'view only' on the learners' side to allowing learners to actually interact with and use the application.

Showing Adobe Photoshop using Application Share

This feature is particularly advantageous when demonstrating software on a one-to-one basis—so it is very popular with IT support/help centres, as well as for use during lessons when you need to demonstrate software applications.

Web browsing

This feature allows the facilitator and/or learners to bring to the class an Internet site or corporate intranet for everyone to view. The facilitator is able to demonstrate websites, but note that learners are just viewing the website that the facilitator has on their screen. A variation of this feature gives control of the web browser facility to each learner allowing them to explore different websites on their own. This valuable resource enables learners to take control of their own learning.

Web browser in action

Breakout rooms

This feature allows the facilitator to create separate breakout rooms for group exercises, in much the same way that you would use syndicate rooms in your classroom sessions. In breakout rooms, learners have access to all of the major facilities of the main room, such as chat, audio, whiteboards and document share (show your presentation slides or share a document). Breakout rooms are ideal for training sessions in which groups can collaborate on specific content in their own rooms. The facilitator can visit each room to provide help and advice—or just listen—and then bring the groups back into the main room.

Managing breakout rooms can be a bit tricky at first, but after some practice you will be able to manage them effectively.

This feature is a great way to achieve group collaboration amongst your learners and you'll find that you will probably use them much more frequently than you would in a classroom environment, with the added bonus that no-one has to walk down the corridor to the rooms—they can be set up almost instantaneously.

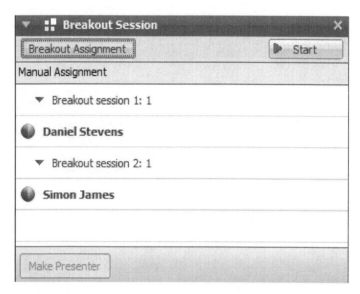

Breakout rooms are probably the most enjoyed and learner-centric facility in the online classroom

Recordings

Most web conferencing software provides the ability to record the session – either to the hosted server or, in some cases, your own computer. Provided the facilitator has recorded the session, this feature allows learners to play back a recording of the session for reflection or further study. This facility also enables learners, who perhaps have missed a session, to play it back at a later date. Another valuable use of the recordings is the ability for the facilitator to assess how the session went and what could have been improved. Some web conferencing systems allow the facilitator to edit the recording to eliminate parts that are not required.

That was a brief walk-through of the main features you can find on web conferencing systems. Gaining mastery of these features is really important for the new online facilitator but takes practice. We shall be exploring and using these features in more depth in later chapters.

How could your organisation use web conferencing systems?

Let's now think about how your organisation could use a web conferencing system to provide learning events for employees. Take a minute to jot down ways in which your organisation could make use of it for meetings, webinars and online classroom events.

Here are a few examples, but note these are just some of the available options.

- **Where face-to-face interaction is not critical**. For some training programmes it is vital that that the trainer is in the same room as the learners in order for the programme to be successful. Lab courses for hardware specialists, where learners physically build computer systems; training in self defence; and wine tasting for beginners, are some typical examples of where web conferencing would not be a good choice. However, in each of these scenarios, some elements of the training would be possible online; so always keep your mind open to reaping the rewards of online learning by combining it with other delivery methods.

- **Where your audience is dispersed throughout a geographic area**. Where learners are not all located in the same place, the online classroom will minimise travel time and save on expenses for travel and accommodation. Therefore, any organisation with locations throughout the country—indeed throughout the world—

would achieve some excellent cost savings using web conferencing systems.

- **Where the topic is sufficiently critical that all employees must complete the training**. Although self-study instruction may be appropriate for teaching the content of, say, Compliance Training, the learners may not be motivated to complete the work. Where a topic is mandatory, using an online event as a follow-up to self-study will provide the impetus for learners to complete the requirements.

- **Where you have a new product or service and you need to update your entire workforce.** Here is a great example of how using the online environment would be invaluable in getting product/service information out to your workforce more quickly and providing some cost savings.

- **Where your work group needs to collaborate**. If you have a geographically dispersed work group that needs to come to a consensus, say to agree the sign-off for a new product, or agree sales targets, you can utilise web conferencing to allow the group to collaborate and share ideas and documents.

- **Where a company official or content expert is available for a specific time**. Let's say that your managing director needs to address all staff on the company's results. By using web conferencing, all staff can see and 'attend' the presentation. This is also true for when, say, a leading expert in your field is available for a particular time on a specific day.

A typical response from some trainers when discussing live online training is that their content is not suitable for teaching in the online environment. With experience you will find that you can design a wide range of effective and interactive online events that you may have previously thought not possible.

Not every topic for every course is best suited to online instruction

We must, however, accept that not every topic for every course is best suited to online instruction. It is important to realise that you should not convert every available course to the online environment just because you can. That said, there are very few courses that could not be adapted in some way for the online environment.

In summary

We saw earlier that organisations throughout the US and Europe are now delivering learning events using the live online classroom environment. Clearly, those organisations are now incorporating it into their learning strategy.

Of those organisations who responded to the e-Learning Guild Survey *Getting Started with Synchronous Systems* (2010), 85% strongly agreed/agreed that "management believes that these approaches are essential to their organisation". Notably, almost 90% stated that they "believed that their live online learning can be as effective as their face to face classroom sessions".

However, there were a couple of significant findings that must be addressed:

- 90.3% strongly agreed/agreed that their online learning tools are not being used to their full potential, and

- 67.9% strongly agreed/agreed that many people in their organisation do not understand the role and benefits of live online learning tools.

In the next chapter, we take a look at the role and skills of the live online learning facilitator.

2

Roles and Skills of the Online Learning Facilitator

Let's now take a look at the role of an Online Learning Facilitator and explore the skills needed to deliver successful learning events.

If you are an experienced and successful classroom trainer then that's great news as you will already have developed a number of core skills that you will call on in the online classroom. Don't be under the impression, however, that all the skills you have gained from your face-to-face classroom experiences will automatically transfer into the online classroom. To be a successful Online Learning Facilitator you will need to learn a new set of skills that you will layer onto your existing ones, and it is this combination that will be your recipe for success.

Here's a good example: let's assume you are already an experienced car driver and you have decided that you want to learn to ride a motorbike. You already have the basic skills required—steering, changing gears, braking, looking in the mirror, road awareness, and so on—but to ride a motorbike you will need to build on those skills and learn an additional set of skills and techniques.

In much the same way that the motorbike rider must build on his existing driving skills, in the online classroom you will need to build on your classroom skills—such as classroom management, handling questions and discussions, and so on—and add a further set of skills specific to delivering live online events. But let's just focus on two of the major new skills you will need in the online classroom. They may not seem like much at first, but believe me they are significant.

Classroom v online delivery skills

There are two key differences between classrooms in the online and offline world. In the online environment you have no visual contact, and you need to master the technology to communicate with and engage participants. Let's look at each of these in turn:

No visual contact

As the famous movie strapline said, "In space no one can hear you scream" and, in the online classroom, you cannot see your learners! For many trainers, the lack of visual contact is the most intimidating feature of delivering in the online classroom.

Through years of experience, trainers are excellent at reading learners' body language. This is used mainly to determine whether the learners are 'getting it' or are getting restless or outright bored (not in your courses, of course!). Trainers use eye contact and body language to assess energy levels; they notice 'cues' that tell them to speed up or slow down; and they look for signals that the learners are paying attention and maintaining interest in the content.

The online facilitator does not have these luxuries and so must rely on other methods to observe learners. But surely if you can't see them, you can't do that; can you?

Just as in real life, when we lose one sense another becomes heightened; so it is with online facilitators. A good online facilitator is able to pick up on all of the cues mentioned despite not being able to see their learners; we will be discussing and highlighting these skills throughout the book.

Using technology to communicate

The second major new skill that has to be learnt is how to manage and 'drive' the web conferencing system such that it is transparent to the learner and does not distract them from the learning; this is a real skill of the online learning facilitator. Getting to know all of the features, and knowing how and when to use them appropriately to facilitate learning, does not come easy—it takes thorough understanding and a lot of practice!

You may think that live online training is limited to teaching technology topics, such as how to use a software application like Microsoft Office.

You may also think that online training cannot match what you can do in the classroom. The reality is that almost anything can be taught in the online classroom. Using the virtual tools, both as they are intended and in creative ways, the facilitator leads the class through a series of activities to achieve the course outcomes. The class can discuss, brainstorm, take notes, work in groups, play content-related games, watch, take part in and control live demonstrations, and so on. Some learning experts contend that the online classroom provides more facilities and scope for learners to learn effectively than does the physical classroom. One of the reasons for this is that the technology provides far more ways for you to engage your learners than can be found in a traditional classroom event.

What other skills will be required?

There are a number of other skills that you will also need. We shall be covering them all in depth in later chapters, but here is a summary of the most important skills:

- **Master your microphone technique**. You will definitely need to master your microphone technique. You must use your voice effectively by keeping it lively, full of energy, pacey, conversational and informal. I liken it to being a radio broadcaster —and that's a new technique for many of us to learn.

- **Keep it interactive and lively**. You need to keep your sessions moving, with frequent interactions and exercises to keep your learners engaged and on their toes. We recommend at least one interaction every 3-5 minutes—this is obviously not cast in stone, but it's worth being aware that you must get learners to do something often. Engage them or lose them!

- **Master your webcam technique.** Using the webcam in a professional manner is another important technique to master. For example, when using your webcam, look straight into it (not your screen) whilst you are speaking. That's not easy to do, but it must be mastered if you want your learners to think you are talking directly to them. Give them plenty of eye contact just as you would in the classroom.

- **Create visual-based slides.** If your slides are currently textual, bulleted lists, and basically PowerPoint defaults, then this must change immediately. The online environment is essentially an audio/visual one, so you need to have visually appealing and in-context slides that include a minimum of text. The use of text-heavy slides is one of the major faults in most of the professional webinars, and switching to visual-based slides is a huge change to make for trainers used to slides full of bullets and text.

- **Sessions should be learner-focused and well-designed.** Your sessions should be learner-focused, not presenter-focused. Once again these may be new skills and techniques to learn. Additionally, your classroom courses will need to be re-designed to incorporate the fast-moving, highly interactive and learner-centred approach if they are to work effectively in the online world.

I have only outlined just some of the main new skills and techniques the classroom trainer must learn to be a successful live online facilitator. We will be covering them all throughout the remaining chapters.

What does the live online facilitator do?

Before we actually drill down into looking at the role a live online learning facilitator performs, let's briefly explore the dual roles the facilitator will play during a typical online session—that is, the roles of instructor and facilitator.

The trainer as instructor

In instructor-mode, the trainer is in control of the learning. The trainer is focused on putting over a pre-determined body of knowledge and skills, directing learner activities, and giving clear instructions on the tasks to be carried out by the learners. The trainer checks the learners' understanding to ensure that learning is taking place. The trainer is also in charge of assessing and evaluating the work of the learners.

In his book *Teaching Today*, author Geoff Petty says that it may seem a paradox at first but this trainer-centred approach has been criticised for being too helpful. Petty says that if you help your learners too much you create 'learned dependency' and 'learned helplessness'—a state of mind in the learners where they believe they are entirely dependent on the trainer in order to learn, and do not have the capacity to help themselves or overcome difficulties unaided.

Consequently, learners fail to take responsibility for their own learning and become passive learners. They go through the motions, doing what the trainer requires, and learn only very superficially. This is also called 'teaching by telling'.

Stuart Box, a lead Facilitator on the IITT's *Certified Online Learning Facilitator* course, has a great term for this style of learning—he calls it 'Lean-back Learning', where the learner leans back in his chair and listens to the instructor. Most webinars, says Stuart, are of the lean-back learning style. However, learner-centred learning, which we shall discuss shortly, he calls 'Lean-forward Learning', where the trainer gives control of the learning to the learners and, by so doing, creates learner engagement rather than passivity.

The trainer as facilitator

Now consider the alternative approach of giving the learners more control over their learning (Box's 'Lean-forward Learning').

This can be accomplished by the trainer 'teaching by asking' rather than 'teaching by telling'.

In the 'trainer as facilitator' approach, the learner takes control of their learning

In the 'trainer as facilitator' approach, instead of the trainer taking control, the learners are given the control over their own learning and so learn to teach themselves. The trainer's role is to facilitate (help and encourage) this process by ensuring that learners really do take control and responsibility. Importantly, help and advice is always given where it is really needed. Let's look at an example of this approach.

Management has asked for a course to explain that the use of social media has been banned at work for 'security reasons'. The trainer begins the session by explaining that, for purposes of security to the organisation's IT system, management has blocked the use of social media by staff. Instead of the trainer using the instructor style of going through a list of the pros and cons of social media in the workplace, the trainer passes control to the learners.

So, the trainer asks the learners a question and tells them to put their views on the whiteboard: *"What are the benefits and challenges of using social media?"* After discussing the learners' responses the trainer poses more questions, such as: *"How can we best ensure that the IT system is kept secure?"*, and *"How could we use social media but ensure the IT system is not compromised?"*, and so on.

Learners are encouraged to think about the problem and provide suggestions/solutions themselves. The facilitator discusses the issues with the group and, by using Socratic questioning techniques, *draws out responses* which will enable the learners to reach a conclusion.

Importantly, the trainer ensures that the learners do as much as possible for themselves. If a learner asks for help, the trainer does not provide it straight away, but uses questioning to guide them to answering their own question. In this way, learners feel a sense of ownership of their learning and are more likely to become active learners during the activity.

Geoff Petty, in *Teaching Today*, asserts that learners often fail to make best progress because of fear, and lack of self-belief.

"Great stress should be placed on developing a supportive psychological climate in sessions. Consequently, facilitators should 'put themselves into their learner's shoes' (develop empathy) and try to become non-judgemental, yet genuine. They should be supportive towards their learners, whom they should hold in high regard as people, however slight their accomplishments."

An important point to learn here is that *only* when the fear of trainer criticism is overcome, is the learner's self-belief developed, which then enables learners to have the courage to take responsibility for their own learning.

Petty provides a great example of this. "Researchers into management styles have compared managers that delegate responsibility to their staff with those who prefer more control. Some managers tell their staff not just what to do, but also how they must do it. Researchers found that the staff of such controlling managers tend to take little initiative, are less committed, and are less creative in finding and solving problems. However, it is found that managers who delegate a good deal of responsibility get much more commitment, creativity and initiative from their staff."

Learners are the same: they tend to take the initiative and develop enthusiasm only when they are given some responsibility and control over their own learning.

Switching styles

Experienced trainers generally favour the facilitator approach in their sessions. However, in practice, there is a continuum between instructor and facilitator, where control over learning is shared, and most trainers move back and forth along this continuum as the situation demands.

They may adopt the instructor style when introducing new material, but switch to the facilitator style when encouraging students to overcome a difficult topic, for example. Like many things in training, the decision is made on the basis of fitness for purpose. However, there is a general consensus that the extreme instructor style, though still common, is not as effective as switching between the two styles. "Becoming a facilitator rather than instructor is not so much about the use of teaching methods. It is an attitude and a set of values," says Petty. Facilitators argue that giving learners more control and responsibility for their learning has the following advantages:

- it encourages active and deep learning, rather than passive and superficial learning

- it discourages a sense of helplessness and dependency amongst learners and encourages the development of self-belief, self-reliance and autonomy

- it is less stressful and more enjoyable for the trainer, who also gains the learners' respect for treating them with respect.

As an online facilitator you will, of course, want your learners to learn effectively, but you may also have overarching personal goals, such as encouraging in your learners:

- curiosity and interest in your subject

- self-confidence and self-belief

- critical-thinking skills and intellectual independence

- creativity, self-expression and personal development

You must, as a facilitator, ensure that your learners achieve the outcomes set for the session but, within these constraints, there is still room to take control and achieve your own vision of good teaching and effective learning.

Carrying out the live online trainer's role

Let's now see what it's like to conduct a live online session. To do that we are going to drop into Michelle's training session.

Michelle is about to run a session about her organisation's new CRM (Client Relationship Management) system. It's an important course as all staff must go through the training before they are allowed to use the new CRM system when it goes live. She has run the course many times before from her base at the Oxford Training Centre and, judging by the way the pre-launch-development CRM system is now being used, she's been successful.

In her sessions, she uses a variety of skills and techniques ensuring that the learners are focused on the learning. Throughout the course she uses her PowerPoint slide deck and utilises a variety of instructional methods and techniques. She also lets each learner have a practice on the CRM system, and she coaches them through using the system.

After the practice session, Michelle puts her group in syndicate rooms where the three groups of four are tasked with discussing what they have learnt and then compiling a list of 'The 5 Golden Rules of Using the CRM System'.

They use the syndicate room's whiteboard to compile their rules. After 20 minutes, Michelle calls them back into the classroom and each group outline their '5 Golden Rules' from their whiteboard.

At the end of the session, Michelle points them to the organisation's LMS where they can download a short e-learning assignment that she's created so that they can learn more about the system and take a short test. She then closes the session, thanks them for their contributions and gives them her contact details in case they have any problems when the go-live date arrives.

So what's so different about this course? Nothing really; it's like any other course that is run all the time. Oh, the only thing that is different is that the sessions are held completely online—sometimes in the evenings. Michelle has not met any of her students—they are based around the organisation's offices in Glasgow, Manchester, Birmingham, London, Swindon, Cardiff, and in the European offices in Portugal, Spain, The Netherlands and Sweden.

Welcome to the world of live online learning!

This morning, Michelle is due to run the session for a new set of learners at 10:00 am. Let's drop in and see what she is doing:

9.00 am: Michelle logs on to her virtual classroom on her laptop on her desk at home. She immediately uploads her presentation slides to check that they are all displaying correctly (including all of the 'slide builds' she uses). She has uploaded two sets of slides—her main presentation slides and her 'Reception Slides', which is a slideshow that is showing on screen when the learners arrive. The Reception Slides comprise a slide with the session name and start time, a slide showing a photo of Michelle, a slide showing how to interact with her and fellow learners (examples of where the response icons and the Chat panel are), a slide reminding learners to switch their phones to mute, and disable any programs running on their computers (except their browser, of course), a slide showing the technical support number should they lose connection, and a slide inviting learners to introduce themselves by microphone, or in Chat if they prefer.

9.10 am: Michelle then logs into the session as a participant using her second computer—this will allow her to see on her second screen exactly what the other learners see—this will highlight any time lags between slides showing on her main computer and the screens of the learners.

9.15 am: With the slides uploaded, Michelle uploads her pre-prepared Polls and loads them all in the Polling panel. She then sets up her pre-prepared Whiteboards that she will be using during the session. Next, she loads some further reading materials that she will let the learners download at the end of the session. She runs a check to ensure that they actually download correctly. She gets the CRM system running on a second browser so that she can show the actual CRM system they will be using (this is called Application Sharing). She minimises the browser until she needs it in the session.

9.30 am: Michelle now sets up the privileges for the Chat and Annotation tools which will enable her learners to write and draw on her whiteboard sessions. Next, she checks out her webcam to ensure that it is working and that there is enough light to show her clearly. Finally, she prepares the Breakout Rooms for the group sessions at the end of the session. Next, she opens up a new browser and logs into a YouTube video she will be showing during her session. She minimises the browser.

9.40 am: The first learner arrives and Michelle switches on her webcam so that the learner can see her. She immediately welcomes them and 'enables' the learner's microphone to check that their audio is working at the right level. As each learner arrives she does the same audio check and encourages those already online to use the microphone or Chat panel to discuss where they are attending from today. She also asks them to put into Chat what they hope to gain from the session. Michelle receives a text from her muted mobile saying that one learner has lost her link for the session. She calls the learner's mobile saying that she will email her a new link immediately. Michelle keeps an eye on the Chat and Participants' panel in case anyone has their 'hand raised' to ask a question. They all seem to be chatting away nicely together.

9.45 am: With seven learners now online and microphones checked, Michelle helps Stephanie who is having a problem with her audio: she explains in direct Chat how to set up the Audio Wizard so that she can set up her audio connection correctly. A hand goes up in the Participants' Panel. *"What can I help you with Alan?,"* asks Michelle. *"My annotation tools are greyed out Michelle,"* says Alan. *"Ah, that's because I haven't given you access rights yet Alan. I will be doing that when we use the Whiteboard."*

9.50 am: The Chat discussion is going well, with everyone contributing and socialising well—there seems to be a couple with a nice sense of humour, helping to 'break the ice', the ice that you sometimes experience when learners are apprehensive. Michelle notices that Stephanie, who had lost her link, has now arrived online. Michelle opens her microphone, welcomes the new learner and checks her audio connection. It's working fine, so Michelle tells the learners that she will be muting their microphones shortly and will be starting the presentation in ten minutes. She also confirms that the session will be recorded. She mutes her microphone and displays her 'coffee cup' icon on screen to show she is away from her desk.

9.55 am: Michelle returns to her desk and de-selects her 'coffee cup' icon. Noticing that the Chat discussion is still going well, Michelle takes a sip of water and opens her microphone to announce the Session Ground Rules, the Session Outcomes and the timetable for the 90-minute session. She then checks that everyone has their phones on silent and that their email and Twitter accounts are disabled. She then switches from the Reception Slide deck to her main presentation slides and mutes the learners' microphones. She starts the session recording by clicking on the 'Record' button. Recording starts successfully.

10.00 am: As ever, Michelle starts her session on time.

At this point, you are probably saying to yourself: "Wow, there is a lot to do all at once, and we haven't even started the session proper yet!". Welcome again to the world of being a live online learning facilitator.

This scenario is based on notes I took whilst co-facilitating one of the IITT's sessions facilitated by Michelle Parish, one of our lead live online facilitators. Did you notice what time Michelle logged on for her 10.00 am session? Yes, it was 60 minutes before course start time. There is a lot to get done in that hour, I'm sure you will agree!

The thing you probably noticed most was the number of different tasks Michelle was carrying out at the same time. This multi-tasking, whilst under some degree of pressure, is one of the most difficult skills that you will need to get used to online. Preparing and setting up a classroom is a breeze compared to a live online session, as I'm sure you can see.

So what role does the online trainer perform? The trainer leads the online classroom event by providing instruction in real time using the Internet and web conferencing software. It is the trainer's responsibility to do the following:

- **Direct the learning**. The session is facilitated to ensure the instructional objectives and the learning outcomes of the session are met.

- **Control the learning environment.** A lot can happen online at once, as we have just seen by following Michelle. For example, if participants are all trying to talk at the same time, or having too many unrelated chat conversations, or are not sufficiently participative, or if the technology fails, the facilitator must find ways to bring everyone back into the fold and prevent confusion.

- **Communicate with participants.** It is easy to overlook participants who are not interacting in the class. The facilitator must pay attention and be sure that everyone is encouraged to participate.

- **Predict participants' needs**. New online participants may need more time to complete activities because of their lack of familiarity with the online classroom environment.

- **Facilitate using collaboration tools**. Long lectures will need to be interspersed with breaks and hands-on activities to split up the sessions. Facilitators must stay tuned-in to maintain the comfort level and keep participants engaged.

- **Encourage interaction**. It is easy for online training to become all about the facilitator, resulting in a passive experience for the participants. Without something to do, every three to five minutes, participants will easily become disengaged. 'Something to do' could mean participating in a chat exercise, answering a question, taking a quiz—in fact anything that keeps participants involved. Be sure that this is more than just 'busy' work with no real purpose. All activities must support and reinforce the instruction (key learning points).

As you can see, in many ways the role of the online facilitator is similar to that of a classroom trainer. However, in addition to these skills, a successful online learning facilitator must be:

- **A participant first**: trainers know what it's like to learn in a classroom setting. We've been doing that all our lives. Most new online facilitators, on the other hand, have not participated in live online training before. So find some online courses, listen to recordings and immerse yourself in the participant experience. How does the dead air make you feel? What do you do when the technology breaks down? What makes an effective exercise question? What did you feel like after sitting there listening to 30 minutes of one-way lecturing?

- **Engaging like a broadcaster**: radio broadcasters project a high energy and speak to their audiences conversationally. They do not need to see the audience to interact with it. Online facilitators also must keep their voices energised and their attitude positive, no matter how many participants are listening. Like the radio broadcaster, you must address the individuals in the group and make your comments personal to them. So use their names often, and talk to them as though they were sitting opposite you.

- **Collaborative**: the online classroom is not the place for the 'sage on the stage'. In order to encourage learning and keep participants engaged, you need to maintain an active part in the process. Online classroom events must be learner-centred!

- **Flexible**: lots of last-minute unanticipated problems can—and often do—occur when working remotely via web technology. Online facilitators must be able to maintain the course flow and manage high-stress situations with grace and professionalism.

- **A multi-tasker**: in a virtual world, facilitators must handle many things at the same time, and it is important to feel comfortable managing multiple tasks simultaneously.

Finally, and probably most importantly, you must be confident and professional—and to accomplish that you must practise as much as possible. You must practise in order to master the web conferencing technology such that the environment is completely familiar to you. You must practise how to deliver your content through this medium, and you'll need to be aware that even the most familiar classroom content will have to be delivered in a different way in the online classroom.

The role of the co-facilitator

There is another important role that needs to be considered when delivering live online events, that is the co-facilitator—often referred to as a Host or Producer.

In normal circumstances, facilitating a small group live online event will usually be conducted by one facilitator but it is not the ideal situation. If you are delivering events that have more than 15 or so, such as a company webinar, then a co-facilitator is vital. Having a co-facilitator on board can make all the difference in producing a successful, professionally delivered event.

So what does the co-facilitator do? What is their role and what typical duties do they perform? Although there are no set down rules, here is a list of tasks that I recommend a co-facilitator carries out in support of the facilitator. Of course, you can compile your own, but these will normally be included.

- **Handling technical issues**. The co-facilitator handles the technical side of the event, leaving the facilitator to concentrate on facilitating the learning. So the co-facilitator will be responsible for any connectivity issues for learners, handling audio set up for the learners and testing that they have connection; ensuring that all the permissions are authorised, for such things as annotation rights and microphone access, and ensuring that breakout rooms are set up ready for the facilitator. Additionally, the co-facilitator should ensure that there is a 'Plan B' should any Internet problems ensue.

- **Ensuring content is available and working**. The co-facilitator should ensure that all content required for the session is loaded and working. So they will upload the session slides, create any whiteboards and polls required, and ensure that any materials for downloading by the learners are uploaded and accessible.

- **Keeping note of the questions asked in Chat or Q&A panels**. The co-facilitator should ensure that all questions entered in the Chat and Q&A panels are answered, preferably in the right order, and should ensure that the facilitator picks these up. Additionally, the co-facilitator can answer questions in Chat whilst the session continues, which adds to the 'flow' of the event.

- **Acting as a 'sidekick'**. There is no doubt that a second voice can make a great deal of difference in a longer session. Interestingly, you will have noticed that many TV programmes now have two presenters. This is because the interplay, banter, and even providing lead lines into a subject certainly enhances the social side of events and breaks up the monotony of just one voice all the time. Of course, the co-facilitator should know the session content too, so they can also contribute to the session by perhaps telling a story related to the topic, so providing an additional viewpoint.

Effective learning events do not happen by accident. Each successful event will have had a great deal of thought, planning and rehearsal carried out well before the actual session itself. So, naturally, your co-facilitator should spend some time rehearsing with you, practising who is doing what and when, and making notes of when these 'hand-offs' to each other occur. During these rehearsals, concentrate on the hand-offs and interplay between you. The more prepared you are, the more successful and professional your live online session will be.

Equipment and facilities you will need

To be a professional live online facilitator, you will need to have some equipment and facilities in place, dedicated to you. So let's discuss the equipment and facilities you will need. In order to present an online session, the facilitator will need a minimum set-up:

A quiet, comfortable place to work. Firstly, you will need a separate workspace—ideally a room which is completely free from outside noise and other distractions. You will definitely need a comfortable chair, plenty of light and a degree of privacy. It needs to be a place where you can sit comfortably for quite a long time. It also pays to remember that bottle of water. I can assure you that you will need it during every session!

Two computers. It is obviously a requirement to have a computer to present from but, ideally, I recommend that you have another on your desk. The second computer should be used as a "learner's" machine—so that you can keep an eye on what your learners are seeing at the same time. This is really useful, especially when you're doing Application Sharing, as the screen refresh on Application Sharing can sometimes lag quite a way behind the main computer. So it is really important to be able to see what the learners' see. On your computer, ensure that all background programs are closed down (not just minimised) and have only the browser running. A note about the quality of your computer. If you are using a laptop, make sure that it's plugged into the mains—experience has taught me never to rely on my laptop batteries. I would recommend a minimum of 2 GB RAM—and preferably more than that—especially if you're doing resource-hungry application sharing or video work. You obviously need a browser to connect to the software, and a reasonable audio card.

Fast Internet connection. You will also need fast broadband connection to the Internet. For presenting online, you need the speed to be the highest it can be for *uploading*. Note, that participants need a fast *download* speed. You can check your broadband connection speeds with various free programs that you can find on the Internet—www.speedtest.com is one example. Although wireless connections are generally good, if you are hosting a session I recommend that your Internet connection be 'hard-wired' via a LAN connection or Ethernet cable. Do not rely on a wireless connection, as this will cause the sound to drop in and out at some stage during the session. Connect your Ethernet cable directly from the wireless router into your computer.

High-quality headset or stand-alone microphone. A good quality microphone/headset is a must—it will make the difference between a successful and an unsuccessful session. If the quality of the audio is poor, the learners will soon switch off. So get the best quality headset you can—they are not expensive and are worth every penny. If you are serious about it, purchase a broadcast microphone and a small mixer. The quality from these professional broadcast products is far superior to the quality you will get from a good headset. Alternatively, if you like walking around when you present, a wireless microphone will do the trick.

Your challenge

Your challenge, as a new live online learning facilitator, is to combine all of your classroom skills and techniques with those outlined in this book to enable you to become the ultimate training practitioner.

So let's now look at how to design your content for the online classroom, and we cover that in the next chapter.

3

Designing your content

Although this book is focused on facilitating live online learning events, I have included this chapter as the majority of online facilitators will also be responsible for designing the content and visuals for their sessions.

All too often it's assumed that you can simply take your classroom course content and use it in the online classroom. This is a huge mistake! Although you can use most of your classroom skills online, your content must be completely redesigned for the online classroom. Notice I say re-designed; you can't just tweak it; it really does need a total rethink.

So why is that?

As you will see throughout the book, facilitating a live online session is completely different from delivering a face-to-face classroom event. Because live online sessions need to be entirely learner-centred and short—less than 2 hours—there are some important points to grasp. These include:

- Having a good understanding of how people learn online

- Focusing totally on the 'need to know'. Put the 'nice to know' in a document or job aid

- Focusing on outcomes (what learners need to be able to *do*, not what they should *know*)

- Developing engaging content which is also absorbing and collaborative

- Ensuring sessions are totally learner-centred

- 'Chunking' topics into small pieces

- Having just one key learning point per slide—ensuring it has impact and connects with the learners personally

- Using web conferencing tools to do the job they are designed for—using them often and mixing them up

This chapter looks at the important considerations in designing an online session. It's not intended as a chapter on instructional design (I'm assuming that you are familiar with how to do that), although we will introduce you to a great model for designing online events—Cathy Moore's 'Action Mapping'. Designing your supporting slides is also a major aspect of designing your session, and we will cover that in more detail in the next chapter.

How we learn

Learning happens when cognitive encoding takes place in the learner—the learner can remember what has been taught (that is, facts, data, principles) by associating it with something that the learner can recall from their memory and which has 'meaning'.

But remember, learning is not just about remembering facts. Would you like a surgeon to perform an operation on you if they had passed their theory exams (the facts) but had not had any experience in actually performing one?

A good example of the cognitive encoding (remember and recall) process is the way London cab drivers undertake their training. In their initial training they need to learn the location of all of the streets, buildings and routes to any destination in the capital (this is known as 'The Knowl-edge'). They acquire this information by practising for many months driving from point to point in the most direct way. By actually driving round the streets from point to point (practising aided by recall of the facts) it reinforces the learning.

Cognitive psychologists believe the process of remembering involves information passing from our brain's Short-term Memory into our Long-term Memory. So, relating this back to how our learners learn, and how we can help them recall information and use it back on the job, we need to understand the basics of Cognitive Load Theory in order to design our sessions. Note that this particularly applies to our slide designs, which we focus on in the next chapter.

So let's look now at Cognitive Load and how it relates to course design.

Memory systems

The human brain has two memory systems: Working Memory (also known as Short-term Memory) and Long-term Memory. These two components complement each other during the learning process.

Learning is the process of taking new information into Working Memory and integrating it with existing knowledge from Long-term Memory. Once it's in Long-term Memory we can recall it and transfer that knowledge into the real world back at work.

Here is some basic information about Working Memory and Long-term Memory:

- **Working Memory**: Your Working Memory is a temporary storage of new information. But that information only lasts for a short time and then is erased. All of your active thinking happens in Working Memory.

- **Long-term Memory**: Whilst Working Memory has a very limited capacity and duration for storing information, Long-Term Memory is basically a repository where you have been storing information since you were born. It has a huge capacity and serves as a permanent store of knowledge. In the learning process, you are connecting the new information to prior knowledge. As you actively process information, you are swapping it between Working and Long-term Memory.

The analogy I use when explaining Working and Long-term Memory is that of a computer. A computer's RAM is the Working Memory and its Hard Disk is the Long-term Memory. The RAM is temporary storage and is limited in size. If you switch off the computer the data is erased. The hard disk is permanent storage—if you switch off the computer, any information stored on the hard disk is retained and, when required, can be retrieved back into your RAM for processing.

The successful outcome of any learning activity is processing new content by transferring information, knowledge and skills from Working Memory into Long-term Memory. As the learner goes through a course, what they see and hear enters their Working Memory where it is stored. The brain then actively processes the new information and integrates it with what they have previously stored in their Long-term Memory.

So the important point here is that the information will only be transferred into Long- term Memory if the cognitive encoding is correct—remember, learning happens when cognitive encoding takes place in the learner— the learner can remember what has been taught by associating it with something that they can recall from their memory and which has 'meaning'. But it doesn't happen automatically. *'If it ain't in, it ain't coming out!'* So, the brain is doing these things:

- receiving new information into Working Memory and accessing Long-term Memory to retrieve any prior knowledge and

- actively processing the information and integrating the information with Long-term Memory information

But your brain has a challenge. Most people can only hold and process a limited amount of data in their Working Memory.

For example, although we could probably solve a simple maths calculation like 12 x 4 in our head, it is not easy solving a calculation like 219 x

473. This is because we have to store information at the same time as processing it.

Your Working Memory has a limited capacity—this is called the Cognitive Load. If you load your Working Memory with too much information, there is no room left to process it. Consequently, it does not get stored in Long-term Memory—so you will forget it. It's much like filling up a glass of water and overfilling it—what cannot be contained gets lost.

So the important lesson to remember is 'never just dump loads of information on your learners', else it will be quickly forgotten.

You have to deliver information in 3 ways:

- **Organise content into small chunks:** Structure new information into small chunks so that it is optimised for Working Memory. If it's not relevant or there is too much information it will interfere with the learning process.

- **Build upon prior knowledge:** Create processes where learners can practise using the information, for example, with the help of practice exercises and case studies—these can help learners integrate the new information with their existing understanding.

- **Provide information with a relevant context:** The goal is to get the learner to pull information out of Long-term Memory and transfer it in a context that is relevant to them back at work.

Cognitive Load Theory

We've seen that Working Memory has a limited capacity for storing information and so we must take great care to not overload it with too much information at once. How can we be sure that we don't do that?

Cognitive scientist George A Miller published some extensive research on this in 1956 which stated that an average human can retain between 5 and 9 objects of information in working memory at one time. Interestingly, recent research (Jeanne Farrington, Performance Improvement Quarterly, 2011) shows that the number is probably around 3 or 4 pieces of information. But you get the picture: Working Memory can retain relatively minimal amounts of information at once. So, in our course design, we must 'chunk' information and ideally repeat it at various intervals to aid recall.

Another leading cognitive scientist, John Sweller, from the New South Wales University, found that all information is passed into our Working Memory through two separate areas—one for visual information and one for auditory information. Visual information is photographs, animations, charts, diagrams, and text; and auditory information is speech.

Sweller says that to increase Working Memory capacity, it is best to combine the visual channel with the auditory channel. So on your slides you would have the image or diagram (visual channel) supported by the explanation in speech (auditory channel)—Sweller calls this 'the modality effect'. Sweller says that "the instructional modality effect occurs when learners, faced with two sources of information that refer to each other and are unintelligible in isolation, learn more when presented with one source in visual mode and the other in auditory mode rather than both in visual mode."

However, my view is that you should not stick rigidly to these findings—research in this area is emerging more frequently now and we are learning about the wonders of the human brain all the time. There is no doubt, though, that we are still at the very early stages of understanding how the brain works.

Session objectives or outcomes?

When designing courses, we are taught that the trainer first decides what they hope to achieve (aims and objectives), then plans the lesson, delivers the lesson (carries out the plan), and then evaluates the lesson to establish whether the set aims and objectives were achieved. This evaluation may lead to change in the aims or content for the next time the lesson runs, and so the process is a continuous circle.

As trainers, you will be well versed in writing SMART objectives (Specific, Measurable, Attainable, Relevant, Time-bound). Aims and objectives are clear and concise statements that describe what the trainer aims to achieve in the lesson or series of lessons. These statements of intent are often expressed in a rather broad and generalised way—for example: "*To improve the learner's ability to conduct a performance appraisal*".

Aims will indicate the general direction in which the trainer wishes to travel. For example: "*The aim of the course is to develop knowledge and understanding of Microsoft Office*". Although they may point you in the right direction, they do not tell you how to get there, or when you have arrived at your destination. So intentions must be described in a more detailed way with what are referred to as 'Learning Outcomes'.

In your sessions, I strongly advocate that you concentrate on learning outcomes, rather than aims and objectives, as they focus on what the learner should be able to 'do' rather than what they should 'know'.

Learning outcomes are *testable statements* that describe what you intend your learners to learn and be able to do—for example: "*By the end of the course, the learner will be able to conduct a Breakout Room session using WebEx Training Centre*".

This is much better than trainer-centred aims such as: "*By the end of the course, the learner will be able to describe how to conduct a Breakout Room session in WebEx Training Centre*".

You will notice that in this case the learner can satisfactorily meet this objective without necessarily ever conducting a Breakout Room session!

So it is vitally important that we shift the focus from teaching to learning. In doing so, it makes clear what the learners have to practise and be able to do, and avoids a lesson dominated by trainer talk, where little real learning takes place. Additionally, if you know precisely what learners should be able to do, it is much easier to assess whether or not they can do it in your evaluation on how successful your session has been.

The crucial point is that the outcomes precisely describe *observable learner performance*, shifting the focus onto what the learners will be able to do as a result of their learning, and away from what the trainer will do. So when designing your live online session, focus on the learning outcomes.

Learner-centred events – guided discovery

Much of your work as a facilitator in the online classroom makes use of the Guided Discovery technique, so it will be really useful to devote some space to it to ensure that you incorporate it into all of your small group learning sessions.

Guided discovery asks the learner to work out the learning for themselves

There are basically two approaches to teaching: 'teaching by telling' and 'teaching by asking'. Teaching by telling is trainer-centred or 'didactic' teaching, where learners have the new learning explained to them; they are then expected to use and remember this new material. Conversely, teaching by asking—also known as the Socratic method—is where the trainer asks questions, or sets tasks, that require learners to work out the new learning for themselves—though usually with some guidance or special preparation by the facilitator. This new learning is then corrected and confirmed by the facilitator.

Guided Discovery is an example of this latter approach, but is only effective if learners are able to think through the new learning using their existing knowledge and experience. Let's look at an example of guided discovery in action.

Case Study: Smarter Mobiles

Jane Banks runs the customer call centre for Smarter Mobiles and is responsible for all of the call centres located throughout the UK. She has been tasked with reducing the response time in dealing with customer queries.

To tackle this issue, Jane runs an online session for her customer support staff and asks her learners what they think would help them reduce the time it is taking to deal with customer queries. She puts them into breakout groups to discuss what could be done to reduce call time, yet still solve the customers' problems. She then asks them to post their findings on the group's whiteboard.

After the group discussion, Jane brings the two groups back to the main room and asks each group to load their whiteboard and present their findings to everyone. Each group presents a list of ways in which they could reduce the time dealing with customer calls.

Alternatively, Jane could have taken the trainer-centred approach and delivered a presentation on the barriers (that she thinks are the cause) and listed some solutions for everyone to write down and memorise.

Which method do you think would help the learners understand what the problems are, how they can improve things, and how they could become more efficient by reducing the response times?

When well-devised and well-managed, the discovery learning method offers active learning and presents a challenge for the learner. Consequently, discovery activities motivate and engage learners, and are also very effective in developing learners' understanding. However, guidance from the facilitator must be given, where necessary, and care must be taken to contextualise the 'problem'. For example, before starting their breakout session, Jane could show her learners the evidence that the response rate for support calls is rising to unacceptable levels and could ask the learners how, as a customer of the company, they would feel about waiting for a long time on the telephone to receive a reply.

It is also important that learners are monitored in their breakout groups. So, as facilitator, you should visit the breakout rooms frequently to ensure the learners are on the right track, and if not, guide them along the right one.

Which topics are best suited to guided discovery?

The best topics for guided discovery are those where reasoning is required, and where learners are unlikely to know the complete solution. Additionally, you need to consider the amount of time you should allocate to discovery. Make sure that you allocate plenty of time for these sessions—about twice as much as you would expect it should take. It is very unlikely that a session of less than 20 minutes will prove to be worthwhile.

And finally, when you have the groups back together, summarise what they should have learnt—this is a really important task and one that you should not miss out. It is crucial that you summarise the main teaching points of the activity, explaining it fully by reference to their findings. The best way to tackle this is to ask your learners what they have learnt.

In summary, the main advantages of the discovery method, used appropriately, are that:

- It is active, involving, motivating, and fun. The questioning element fosters curiosity and intrinsic interest in the subject matter.

- Learners must find their own meaning—that is, create their own understanding of the subject matter. Consequently, they'll understand it and be able to link it to their prior learning. It is the pre-eminent constructivist method of learning.

- Learners are likely to remember what they worked out for themselves.

- It involves learners in high-order thinking: evaluation, creative thinking, problem solving, analysis, synthesis, and so on.

Discovery learning provides learners with the satisfaction of solving problems for themselves and so, arguably, it develops their intrinsic as opposed to their extrinsic motivation. But, as in much group work, there is a danger that some learners will watch rather than participate. You can, however, avoid this situation by asking each learner to take on a role in the breakout room, such as leader, whiteboard scribe, controlling the microphones, responsible for saving the whiteboard at the end of the session, and so on.

Guided discovery is fun; it is motivating and it develops the learners' thinking skills. It is a natural way to learn—children and animals spontaneously learn this way, so it fits with the way our brain has evolved.

Action Mapping: a model for instructional design

There are numerous models for developing learning—two of the most used in instructional design circles are ADDIE (Analysis, Design, Development, Implementation and Evaluation), and Gagne's behaviourist/cognitivist 'Nine Events of Instruction'—but my preference is to base your online classroom session designs on a relatively new method, Action Mapping, which has been developed by e-learning design expert Cathy Moore.

When I attended a webinar by Cathy on Action Mapping last year it was a bit of a 'light bulb' moment for me as far as instructional design was concerned. I had found a method that was completely learner-centric, was simple to understand, and provided a framework to help you design business goal-oriented results for your sessions. In turn, it ensures that your sessions deliver what learning is supposed to—a change in behaviour and aligned to business performance improvement.

Action Mapping is a streamlined instructional design process that will help you identify the most powerful activities for your online learning project, ensure that excess information is eliminated from your sessions, and will support measurable performance improvement for your learners and the organisation.

The Action Mapping approach will help you to:

- Pinpoint the measurable performance improvement that your session will help create

- Identify why people aren't performing as required and how your session could help improve their performance

- Create compelling, realistic scenarios that motivate learners and let them learn by doing

- Eliminate the information they don't need

- Identify what information should go in job aids and other easy-to-update support materials

Cathy Moore explains that a lot of today's online/e-learning courses are nothing more than information dumps. She says that learners are getting too much information—most of it irrelevant to what they need to do their jobs. Information dumps equal cognitive overload and this makes learners bored, uninspired and passive. "We are giving them information but we are not helping them to learn. We think information will help them change their behaviour—it won't," she says.

Cathy says that we typically give learners long lists of facts to learn and then create a test to see if they have remembered them. All we are testing is Short Term Memory recall. It is not learning.

The goal of Action Mapping is to design 'experiences'. We need to help learners to practise making decisions that they need to make on the job. So you need to set a measurable business (not learning) goal for your session. You need to show how you will improve business performance to justify the expense of your session. So you need to identify what people need to do in the real world to reach the goal and determine why they are not doing it at work. Lack of knowledge about a subject may not be the problem!

Cathy says that you should create activities that enable learners to practise making the decisions that they will need to make in their job. "Making them recite them [the decisions] will not do it," she says. "Show the realistic consequences of making those decisions and let learners draw conclusions from them. Success in the decision-making activity shows that the learners have learnt—so there is no need for fact checks, which are simply testing recall from their Short-term Memory not the ability to actually carry out the procedure."

In explaining the Action Mapping model, Cathy says "surprise and failure are memorable, so let learners make mistakes—they will remember them. And make sure everything in your session supports the business goal. Cut out everything that does not do that."

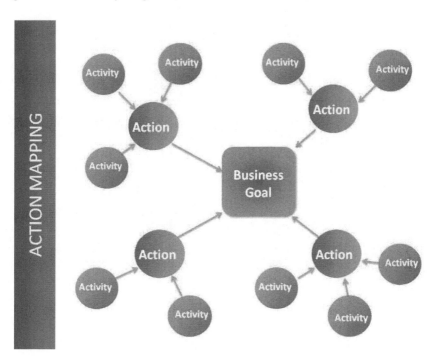

So, to design your sessions using Action Mapping you should follow these four steps:

- **Identify the business goal**—choose a goal that leads to a measurable business improvement—for example, "Answer all customer enquiries in 15 seconds or less."

- **Identify what Actions people need to do to reach that goal**— list realistic 'Actions' that help learners apply their new knowledge on the job to meet that goal.

- **Design Activities that help people practise each Action**—for each 'Action', design an 'Activity' that helps people practise that 'Action' ensuring it mirrors the workplace environment.

- **Identify the minimum information needed to complete each activity**—only use information that people must have to complete each activity. Decide what information should go in a session and what should go in a job aid.

By following these four simple steps, everything is focused on supporting the business goal that you have set.

So now you have your Action Map as a development plan for your session. Let's look at a scenario that will help demonstrate how to use Action Mapping in your sessions:

Case Study: Penn Stores

Alan Davies is the manager of a small suburban store selling convenience goods from 7.00 am to 11.00 pm. He has a staff of eight people who work in two shifts. During the evening shift, the store is mainly manned by women. As Alan is normally only on site during "normal" working hours, the evening staff often work without a manager present.

During the last 12 months the store has been robbed four times and there have been six instances where staff have been threatened with violence. Each time these events have happened on the evening shift when Alan was not present.

The company HR department wants to ensure that all store managers follow the company's Security Procedures and Processes manual and are conversant with ways to minimise danger to their staff. HR has asked for an online course to be developed to address these issues. As a basis for this course, HR has provided a list of documents which set out the rules for staff who work in their stores.

In a typical course, the content would be something like:

- About this course

- What is workplace violence?

- Risk factors

- Violence prevention procedures

- Types of security controls

- Post incident forms

- Sources of assistance

This is a classic information dump course. Instead of looking at the information that this course would provide, let's take a look from the learner's perspective. Rather than sitting through a 'teach and tell' online course, which goes through the company's security rules and procedures manual, let's look at how the Action Mapping 4-step model will provide the results.

Step 1: Create Measurable Goals

Firstly, we need to move away from a goal that is totally information-based ("*Store Managers will be conversant with the company's Security Procedures and Processes manual*") to a business goal that is measurable and related to the learners' perspective. From our scenario, Alan Davies's goals are to stop the incidents of the robberies and threats which are putting his staff in danger. We need to produce a measurable business goal for the session, perhaps something like: "*Eliminate situations which would put staff in danger of violence or threat in all stores within 3 months.*" So we have moved from a goal all about 'Information' to a business goal all about 'Action'—it actually measures change in the workplace, which is what learning should be about, right?

Step 2: Identify what people need to do

Having set the measurable business goal, we need to identify the Actions that will lead to this goal. So, what actions can Alan take? Perhaps the list would be: increase staff presence between 7.00 and 11.00 pm; ensure cash is transferred from the cash register to the safe every hour; investigate the installation of CCTV both inside the store and in the car park; consider installing an emergency buzzer that is linked to the local Police station; encourage staff to report suspicious behaviour; investigate whether it is possible to increase the power of the floodlights in the car park, and so on. These are all actions that Alan can do on the job. Note that all of these Actions are directly related to the business goal.

Step 3: Design activities to get them to practise doing what they need to do

For each Action, you must include a practice activity. So you need to design an Activity that helps learners practise the Action. Each activity should mirror the workplace, so we could create role plays, scenarios, possibly games or simulations for each Activity.

Step 4: Identify what people really need to know

Obviously some information is necessary and needs to be memorised, but ensure that it is only the essential information for each activity. This is information that the learner must have to complete an activity. If the piece of information does not support the practice activity do not use it! So what information does Alan need to know to be able to complete the Activities? Let's say it would be perhaps emergency procedures in case of incident, basic principles of security, how to ensure the safe is secure, how to ensure CCTV tapes are changed, ensure staff are not alone in high risk times, and so on.

The details of this information as well as other information can be provided as job aids—for example, checklists and information sheets for Alan to be able to ensure vital procedures have been undertaken, replace faulty floodlight bulbs, test the emergency buzzer connection to the Police station, and so on.

Using the Action Mapping 4-step model, you now should have a document outlining the business goal, the associated Actions that must be done, and the associated Activities for each Action. You now need to think about how to take each Activity on your list and create an exercise to enable the learners to practise it. Remember to keep revisiting your business goal to ensure that the activity you are working on is fulfilling that. You now need to decide how accomplish the Activity using the web conferencing facilities that you have at your disposal—such as breakout rooms, whiteboards, polls, and so on. But be careful to ensure that the technology supports the Activity rather than using it 'because it is available'.

Many of the Activities will undoubtedly use either the breakout rooms or whiteboard, as these are best for group activities. So, for example, in our scenario on the convenience store, you could conduct a role play exercise to practise how to handle an aggressive customer, or perhaps you could use the whiteboard to gain everyone's suggestions for ways to increase security on the premises after 9.00 pm.

The value of these collaborative tools in the online classroom is that they are inclusive—that is, they provide equal opportunities for everyone in the group to contribute, work and learn from each other.

It may be that in designing learning events you have to use a prescribed instructional design model, so of course you will need to follow that. However, I urge you to try out the Action Mapping model on one of your sessions so that you can see the benefits it brings to the learners' and the organisation's performance.

In summary

In this chapter on designing your session, we have covered a lot of information that you need to take into consideration when you design a session for the online classroom. Specifically, we have taken a look at how the human brain takes in information and how we should avoid situations of cognitive overload at all times. As we highlighted, this is even more important in the online learning environment than in the face-to-face classroom.

We have discussed, when you are designing your sessions, whether to use objectives or learning outcomes, and have taken a look at using guided discovery learning and the benefits it provides, especially in live online events.

Finally, we looked at a learner-centric model of designing online learning (whether it's an e-learning course or a live online learning session)— Cathy Moore's Action Mapping. This simple-to-understand 4-step model eliminates the need for 'information dump' presentations and instead concentrates on designing experiences, focused on learners' needs, which are targeted at the business change goal of the session.

Now we need to look at another aspect of online learning design—the importance of designing your visuals with the same goals in mind. And that chapter is next—Designing Your Slides.

4

Designing your slides for the online classroom

As the old saying goes, a picture paints a thousand words, and there's almost no place where this has greater application than with live online learning events. As the audience generally can only hear you, but can't see you, the impact of the visual elements (your slides) is critical in attracting learners to the content and maintaining their engagement throughout. In this chapter we will explore your visual collateral and the importance of having engaging visual content.

I attend many conferences and courses—both in the classroom and online—and it is a sad fact, but the standard of slides used by most presenters and trainers is poor. We have all seen slides that are full of bullet-pointed text, with the text crammed in making the point size so small that it is unintelligible. This must change if we want our learners to learn.

So why are the majority of the presentation slides we see poor? Is it because, as trainers, our development is centred on the delivery side of things—we focus on developing our delivery skills, and our slides are there as support for our script. In many cases, the presenter's slides are the actual script itself! How often have you seen the presenter reading from their slides on the screen?

A typical bullet-point slide (including decorative but meaningless clipart)

The fault is not necessarily the trainer's, however. The problem is that the value provided by well-designed and well-thought-out slides, in enabling learning to take place, is largely ignored when we are taught how to deliver learning or give a presentation. I researched many books on how to give presentations; only a handful of them even touch on how to design good supporting slides.

Think back to when you were taught how to deliver training. Were you ever taught the basics of good presentation slide design? I very much doubt it. I would also contend that few people have received any Power-Point training, let alone training in basic slide design. Today's software applications are designed to get users up and running with minimal (if any) training. So it's not necessarily all down to the trainers—you don't know what you don't know!

I would like to see 'train the trainer' courses of the future include basic presentation graphic design skills and basic PowerPoint (or an alternative slide development program like Keynote or Prezi) presentation software skills. Maybe then we can eliminate 'Death by PowerPoint' slides.

Another reason that the majority of presentation slides are poor is that most courses and presentations are actually developed using PowerPoint as the starting point. Let me explain. Trainers have their content mapped out (or prescribed for them) and they start producing their slides using PowerPoint's default layout of bulleted lists. (I did this many times when I was a trainer). They may add in some default clip art that comes with the software, change the background colour or theme perhaps, and reduce the text size so that all the words fit on the slide.

So is it any wonder that we see the same format set of slides in nearly every course or presentation?

Cognitive load and visuals

Before we start looking at slide design principles, it's important to understand how the brain deals with visuals in the learning context. We saw in the previous chapter that we must take care not to overload our learner's Working Memory by dumping too much into it in a short period of time. Let's look at the issue of Cognitive Overload Theory with respect to visuals.

John Sweller, from the University of New South Wales, and one of the foremost experts in cognitive science and learning, produced research on this subject (*Visualisation and Learning*). Sweller says that Working Memory comprises two separate areas—one for Visual information and one for Auditory. When we explain a key learning point using a slide, this information is passed into the learner's Working Memory through their eyes (the slide content) and ears (the accompanying speech).

So there are two channels (or highways) of data—one for visual elements and one for auditory.

In order to help the learner retain information, therefore, we should never mix two visual items or two auditory items. This means that it is most efficient to show a slide (visual channel) and explain the key learning point (auditory channel).

So to avoid overloading our learners' Working Memories, never repeat text that is on the slide. Now how many of us do that? How many courses have you seen with the bulleted text on the slide being read by the presenter? I would guess you are saying 'most, if not 'all'.

The power of images

Images are one of major tools used to engage learners, communicate content, convey instruction, and promote active learning. Research from Dr John Medina, in his book *Brain Rules*, shows that people learn better from pictures *and* words than from words alone—which is not surprising considering that the majority of our sensory input is visual.

Dr Medina found that presentations that rely predominantly on text alone fail to engage and teach as effectively as appropriate visual representations. Alternatively, slides that incorporate too many decorative pictures that are unrelated to the content will hinder the learning experience.

So it's all a question of balance. We need to concentrate on developing our skills to produce high-quality visuals that enhance the learning experience of our learners.

Let's now look at how the brain interprets visuals. I was first introduced to this by one of the leading authorities on instructional design and learning, Neil Lasher when I attended one of his courses on e-learning instructional design. He asked: "When you first look at any visual (photograph, poster, slide) what do your eyes do? According to the revered newspaper designer, Edmund Arnold (1913-2007), our eyes follow a certain pattern that is wired in the brain. He called it the Gutenberg Diagram".

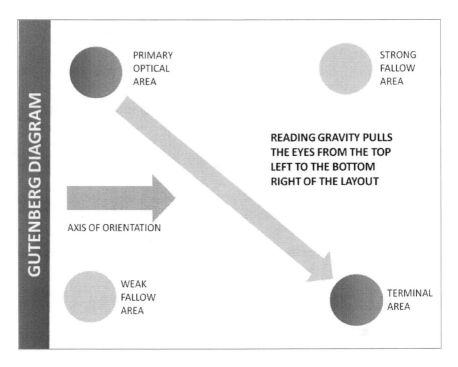

When we are taught to read, we are told to start at the top left corner of the reading matter and work our way across and down, going from left to right and back again, until we reach the bottom right corner. Arnold says the eyes fall naturally to the top left corner, which he calls the Primary Optical Area. Then, the eyes move across and down the page, obeying reading gravity, and returning after each left-to-right sweep to an axis of orientation. This will, of course, take a matter of milliseconds.

So we need to use this information when designing visuals.

Fundamentals of graphic design

Now I know you may be thinking, "I'm no good at designing things". How-ever, there are only a few basic rules to follow and, if you can understand them and use them in your slide design, then you will have slides that will do the job that we – or more appropriately, your learners – need. If you are interested in the basics of graphic design, I recommend an easy to understand explanation on Garr Reynolds's blog on presentation design (http://www.garrreynolds.com/Design/basics.html); Garr, I believe, is the master of slide design for effective learning.

Here are some other excellent examples from people who have mastered the art of slide design, and I recommend that you have a look at them.

- The Presentation Secrets of Steve Jobs: How to Be Insanely Great in Front of Any Audience by Carmine Gallo

- Presentation Zen: Simple Ideas on Presentation Design and Delivery (Voices That Matter) by Garr Reynolds

- slide:ology: The Art and Science of Creating Great Presentations: The Art and Science of Presentation Design by Nancy Duarte

- Resonate: Present Visual Stories That Transform Audiences by Nancy Duarte

- Beyond Bullet Points by Cliff Atkinson

- Better Than Bullet Points by Jane Bozarth

Slide content design: Assertion/Evidence Model

I discovered a great method of designing slides from one of my favourite presentation design experts, Olivia Mitchell of Speaking About Presentations. She introduced me to a clear and structured model of how to design presentations—the Assertion/Evidence model—which was designed by Professor Michael Alley of Penn State University.

In the Assertion/Evidence model you need to map out every key learning point that you want to transfer to your learners. This is called your Assertion statement. For every Assertion, you need to provide the explanation (or evidence). You can do this using an explanation, a story, or statistics, for example.

When you are compiling your Evidence, you need to be careful not to fall into the Death by PowerPoint trap by adding loads of text to your slides. If you have a few evidence statements that all tie in with the Assertion statement you can list them, but keep the list to less than 5 and keep the number of words to a minimum (say, 5/6 words). So using our story on Virtual Airlines below, let's create a new slide for each Assertion, and provide a maximum of 5/6 words for each Evidence statement.

The chairman of Virtual Airlines (VA) needs to make a presentation to his employees about the budget cuts he has had to make during the economic downturn. Over the next five years, they aim to save £22m through reducing the workforce by 10%, cut routes to South America and the Far East, and dispose of subsidiary companies not core to the business. Besides the staff cuts, there is a recruitment freeze, and early retirement packages and cut sabbatical leave stopped.

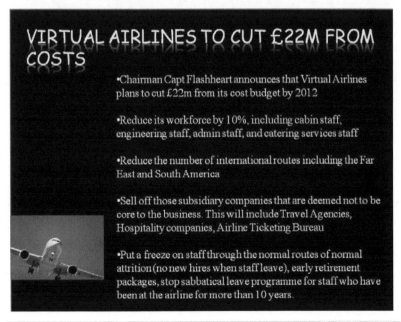

This slide is basically a bullet-pointed script for the presenter, with a meaningless decorative photograph. We've all seen hundreds of these types of slide, haven't we? How on earth can we expect our audience to take all of that in? Cognitive overload in action!

So let's look at how it should be done—to enable the audience to understand the key messages—by applying the Assertion/Evidence model. Firstly, let's create a title slide. We will need a photograph that has impact, portraying an airline from the Virtual Airlines fleet. We then need a short, snappy and to-the-point title.

The Title slide – the headline of the presentation

In the title slide we have used an image of a Virtual Airlines aircraft, which connects immediately to the story and is the hook for the audience, outlining the key message.

Now we need to write down an Assertion statement for each point that the chairman will be going through in his presentation. Once we have our

Assertion statements we need to provide Evidence statements. Here are my suggestions for the first two points:

Assertion 1: Securing our future
Evidence 1: Some necessary but painful cuts needed

Assertion 2: Reduce our workforce
Evidence 2: We need to cut workforce by 10% by 2016

And so on.

Let's now compile our next slide. Our Assertion is 'Securing our future' and our Evidence is 'Some necessary but painful cuts required'.

Slide 2: Securing our future (the first Assertion)

In slide 2, we see the **Assertion** (Securing our future) and the **Evidence** (Some necessary but painful cuts required).

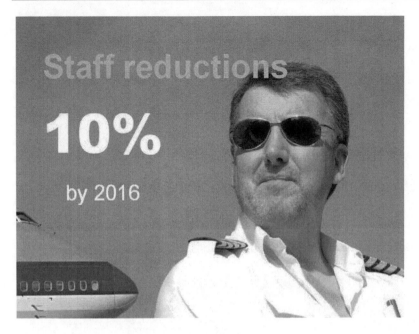

Slide 3: Staff reductions (the second assertion)

In slide 3, note the **Assertion** (Staff reductions) and the **Evidence** (10% staff cuts are needed by 2016).

If you design your presentation using this model, you will have a clear, structured and easy-to-take-in presentation that your audiences will understand and remember.

I hope you'll give the Assertion/Evidence model a try and adopt it in your presentations.

Choosing the right visuals for the job

It's a well-known fact that Vision is our most powerful sense. Therefore, designers use visuals to grab the audience's attention to help them understand and remember the content. A powerful image can make or break a design. Photographs, illustrations and artwork are used to tell stories, support ideas and hold the audience's attention; so the selection of the right visual is important.

One of the world's experts in how the human brain works, Dr John Medina, says that vision trumps all of our other senses. His research found that we have a better recall of images than text. "Hear a piece of information and 3 days after you will remember just 10% of it. Add a picture and you will remember 65% of it," he says.

Dr Medina's studies have found that recognition of a topic doubles if you use a picture compared with just using text. "This is because reading text is inefficient for us. We have to read text on a slide and that takes time," he says. So the message is—you can use text for 'understanding' on a slide but you must keep those words to a minimum.

Photographs also give your learners an emotional connection with the message you are trying to convey. Your slides need to tell a story and connect emotionally with your audience—and the best way to do this is to use photographs. They draw your audience, make emotional connections, and prepare your learners for what you have to say.

As a 'presenter', the first thing to understand is that your learners want to listen to you—not read your slides. Otherwise, you might as well send them a document to read, right? So, the aim is to use your slide to fill your learners' minds with an image, and then fill in the details of what you have to say.

Your visuals can be a variety of things: photographs, charts, diagrams, animations. Let's look at these and see how we can use each type of visual to enhance your message.

Photographs

Professionally taken photographs can really enhance the overall quality perception of your presentation. Choosing the correct photograph for the point you're making is of prime importance. You need to choose your photograph very carefully, so think very hard about the concept you're trying to put over and how best to represent it with a photograph. If the viewer can't see the context and relevance, it can hinder the learning.

As a general rule, do not use Clip Art, as it appears cheesy, amateurish and out-dated. If you found your image in the clip art library that came with PowerPoint, your audience has seen it hundreds of times. Hardly going to make them sit up and listen to you, is it?

Sourcing quality images may seem like quite a hurdle, but I encourage you to think about taking your own photographs to tell the story. Today's digital cameras are fine for taking good quality photographs. Let's say you wish to present an induction programme for new entrants to your organisation. You could take photographs of the Chairman or MD, the management team, the main office locations they need to be aware of, and a photograph of where everyone should assemble for a fire drill, for example. Be creative! Besides saving money by not using stock photographs, the benefit of taking your own is that they will be more meaningful and relevant to your learners.

For other presentations, you could use quality photographs from stock photo sites. There are hundreds of stock photo sites on the Web—some are paid for and some are actually free, usually as long as you credit the photographer on your slide.

The important point, though, is that the photograph you use must be high-quality and of a sufficiently high resolution and size that it is crystal sharp when displayed on screen. If you resize a small or low-resolution photograph, it will be blurred and have jagged edges. Please avoid them at all costs.

So always use high-quality images and graphics of a good size and resolution, such as those available on the professional stock photo sites. I have provided a list of good sites in the Resources section. You may be surprised at how inexpensive these photographs are. Two examples of sites I use are *bigstockphotos.com* and *istockphotos.com*, where you can purchase a high-quality graphic photograph or illustration for between £1 and £5.

Whenever you use photographs that you have not taken yourself, you should pay attention to the copyright that is attached to the particular photographs you use. Read the small print carefully and abide by the rules diligently. If you are unsure, it's always best to ask the photographer's permission—they are normally pleased to grant you permission to use their images as long as you credit them with a link to their website or blog.

Here are some tips on using photographs on your slides:

- **Make the photograph as large as possible.** Large photographs make an impact, so make your photograph full size or as large as you can on your slides. A small, token picture to fill up a gap on the slide is worthless and merely decoration—in fact it is worse than that, as it can hinder the learning by filling up short-term memory with an irrelevance.

- **Use people in images with care.** Be careful with positioning people on your slides. You need to ensure that their eyes are looking into the centre of your slide—do not have them looking out of the slide, as your audience will instinctively follow the direction of the gaze of a person in the photograph.

- **Line drawings, silhouettes, and symbols are often a good solution**. For maximum clarity, keep the background plain and simple.

- **Animations can be helpful in explaining processes, but they shouldn't be used for effect.** They can actually impose an increased mental load on the learner because they can impart a great deal of visual information in a transient manner.

Choose photographs very carefully—think hard about the concept you want to put over. Look for a metaphor or analogy that describes the message. Look for photographs that tell a story, and match visuals with the context of what you are describing. If the learner can't see the context and relevance it can hinder the learning because your learners will waste brain power by figuring out the relevance.

There really is no excuse for some of the awful photographs and images that we see every day on presentation slides. So do something about it and learn some more about presentation design. I can recommend any of Garr Reynolds's books, which you can find on Amazon. Of particular interest will be *Presentation Zen Design*. It changed my life as far as slide design is concerned. There is a complete list of books on slide design in the Resources section.

Graphs and charts

When you want to use graphs and charts on your slides, the key is to keep it simple and make your point clearly. We all use graphs and charts in our presentations, and most people create a graph in MS Excel and paste it into their slides. I advise you not to use this method. Here's a typical pie chart that has been created that way—you see charts like this all the time.

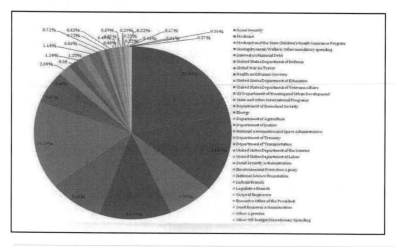

In this example (an actual slide from a presentation I was given), the presenter was outlining that the particular country's Government spent more on its Defence than its Education and Health and Welfare services combined.

I'm sure that unless the presenter explained it to the audience, no-one would have grasped the key point from the visual at all. So you need to keep your charts and graphs simple and only show or highlight the key learning point you want to make. I can guarantee that, if you follow this advice, the point is more likely to stick in your audience's memories.

So what do I mean by 'keep it simple and to the point'? Here's an example of a slide I designed for a study on the daily consumption of coffee by the population of the world. The point being made was that, in the UK, coffee consumption is fairly minimal compared with the US and France (the two largest consumers of coffee).

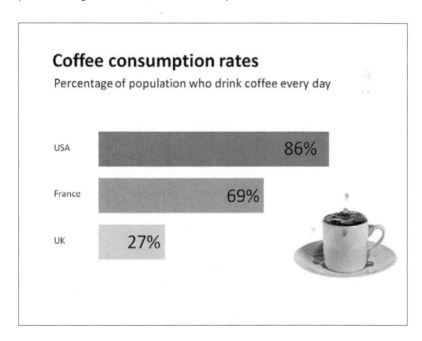

Now, I could have put every country in the survey on the chart—but that was not the point I wanted to make. So I chose only the relevant countries, and produced a clean and simple chart that actually made the point I needed to get across. I could have produced a hand-out of the full results for learners to see the whole set of data but, on the slide itself, I'm sure you'll agree there was no need for that information.

So, when you show data, concentrate on the key learning point and eliminate the unnecessary information. Keep the colours balanced—and include a visual if you think it helps make the key learning point.

For those of you who want to explore displaying effective graphics and charts, I can recommend *Information is Beautiful* by David McCandless, and books by Edward Tufte. In particular, Tufte also has a very short 'brochure', aimed at PowerPoint users, showing how to approach slide design.

Using text and type

We have already seen that we need to eliminate as much text as possible on our slides. What text you do put on your slides should be succinct and making a key learning point. Remember, we do not want explanations (that's your job!).

Some people question the need for text on slides at all. So do we need text on slides?

Olivia Mitchell believes that slides are more effective with pictures *and* words for most business presentations. Here are 3 reasons she provides:

- A photograph can be interpreted differently by different people. Adding a clarifying short statement ensures that everyone gets the point you are making.

- You can highlight a certain key point by just having one statement on a slide. This is also useful for people whose first language may not be the same as yours.

- Quotations are best with the words on the slide. Most audiences find it useful to read a quote rather than hear it.

We have already discussed that Working Memory processes visual and audio, so remember you should only use a maximum of one audio and one visual channel on any slide.

It is vitally important, then, that you do not just read out the text on your slides. It's difficult for participants to take in the audio from the presenter at the same time as reading the text on the slide. Research from Dr John Medina says that participants are more likely to read the text than listen to the audio—so you'll find that they won't be listening to what you're saying; they'll be reading. Additionally, people can read faster than the time it takes to say it—so they'll be waiting for you to finish!

So let's explore how to eliminate unnecessary words to end up with a succinct but clear statement for our slides. Some people have an in-built ability to edit a set of words—I am fortunate in this case as my previous career was a magazine publisher and editor, so editing (or 'red penning' as it is called), comes easy to me. If you have not tried it, I am sure that if you follow some rules you will be proficient at it too.

So here is the statement that's far too long for a slide (22 words):

> "The facilitator should welcome each person who logs in by their name to make them feel part of the community of learners."

So how could we cut that sentence down to retain the key learning point?

Firstly, highlight the key words (those that must be there).

> "The facilitator should welcome each person who logs in" — this could be shortened to "**Welcome participants**"

> "by their name to make them feel part of the community" —this could be shortened to "**by name**".

So we have cut the long 22-word statement down to four words and retained the key point:

"Welcome participants by name"

Now, which one is easier to remember?

Another valuable tip when you are presenting, whether online or not, is to introduce the slide's text before you show it on the screen. If you show it first, your learners will read it and will not be listening to you. So, when you display your slide which contains text, keep silent for 2-3 seconds to allow your learners to read it before you speak to avoid any listening/reading conflict.

Fonts and typefaces

Now let's consider the choice of font/typeface that you use on your slides. This is an important subject because to choose a font that is difficult to read will hinder the learning; so we need to select fonts that are reader-friendly, especially when projected on a screen.

So where should you start? Well, there are hundreds of fonts available, but you should preferably choose a font that is easy-to-read and looks 'modern'.

Fonts come in two styles: Serif and Sans Serif.

- Serif fonts are those with the additional bits added at the top and bottom (they are called 'serifs'). **Times New Roman** is an example of this.

- Sans Serif fonts are those that are 'clean' without the tops and tails of Serif fonts. **Arial** is an example of a Sans Serif font. (Sans Serif means 'without serifs').

- Sans Serif fonts have become the de-facto standard for text on-screen, especially in the e-Learning and online environment. This is partly because the interlaced display of computer screens may show flickering on the fine details of the horizontal serifs. Additionally, the low resolution of digital displays in general can make fine details like serifs disappear or appear too large.

Of course, the decision about which font to use may not be in your hands as you may be restricted by your organisation's house style but, if you can choose your own font, go for the more modern-looking fonts like Verdana, Helvetica, Arial, Tahoma and Gill Sans. Although it's a Serif font, Century Gothic is also a good font because of its shape and spacing, and is recommended by the British Dyslexia Association (more about them in the section on colour).

Whatever font you choose, I recommend that you use the same font family for your entire presentation—you can use different font weights (like Arial Black and Arial) but for a nice, clean, professional look do not mix fonts. My preference is for Helvetica Bold for headings and Helvetica for any standard text.

And finally, ensure your text size is large enough to be seen clearly when viewed in a relatively small window in your online classroom. Files that, previously, you may have projected on a large screen may not be large enough on the smaller online classroom window. Keep the text font and font size consistent throughout your session—28 pt minimum and 32 pt or larger are ideal. Settle on one size for headings and one size for the body text.

Using colour

Now let's look at using colour on your slides. The use of colour is a huge topic, but these are the main points to consider when choosing a colour scheme for your presentation slides.

Colour can be used to emphasise, get attention and point the way, but it is also emotional, according to Garr Reynolds, author of the excellent *Presentation Zen* books. So using the 'right' colour is an important choice when designing your presentation slides—or any screen-based learning for that matter.

Different colours are associated with feelings and, according to Reynolds, can be very culture-specific; therefore interpretation can vary depending on your audience. But there are some generally accepted associations, both negative and positive. Correct usage relies on finding out about your audience in order that you can choose appropriate colours—and of course those to avoid. Furthermore, quite a few people are 'colour blind', so you should take that into consideration too.

In his book *Presentation Zen Design*, Reynolds provides a list of typical colours and their emotional connection:

- **Red**: assertive, powerful, bold, urgent, intensity, emotionally hot, love and passion

- **Pink**: romantic, soft, tranquil, passive, femininity, health, love, romance, joy

- **Orange**: warmth, compassion, excitement, enthusiasm, spiritual, energised, fun

- **Green**: natural, balance, harmony, environment, earthy, healthy, persistent, calm

- **Blue**: dignified, professional, successful, loyal, calm, peaceful, tranquil, positive, authoritative

Once again, you may be obliged to use your corporate colours—but if not, why not think about the message you want to put over, and connect with your audience's emotional side?

Choosing the 'right' colour is important—indiscriminate use of colour looks awful. I have seen yellow text on a lime green background, honestly. At best it may annoy and distract from the key learning point: at worst it can cause headaches or eyestrain. So ensure that you have an overall colour theme for your presentation; do not mix colours for your text, and only use black or dark text colour on a light backgrounds. Note that you can use dark backgrounds of course, but make sure the text colour is readable. Black backgrounds are better than white when you are projecting your slides in a large room, like at a conference. White backgrounds can glare and cause eyestrain in large conference rooms. My advice for online learning is to use only primary and secondary colours and, wherever possible, keep the background simple, and ideally white.

Finally on colour, as already mentioned, you should take into consideration that you may have learners who are dyslexic or colour blind. If this is a consideration for you, I suggest you look at the British Dyslexia Association website where there is a useful guide for slides and the Colour Group website for those who are colour blind. You can find the website links for both of these sites in the Resources section.

In summary

In this chapter we have focused on designing slides that have one purpose—to ensure your key learning points are conveyed to, and retained by, your learners through not overloading their Working Memory.

My final plea is to ditch the irrelevant clutter on slides. There is absolutely no need to display slide numbers and, apart from perhaps the first and last slide, there is no need to put the company logo on every slide (unless your corporate policy dictates otherwise).

As Garr Reynolds says, "White space is beautiful" and I totally agree with him. Do not clutter up your slides by filling them up with irrelevant 'junk'.

5

Preparing your session

As with all major projects, the success of the final outcome depends on how well you have planned the project. Building and delivering online events takes a lot of preparation but, with practice, you can create excellent and effective learning experiences. If you prepare correctly, you should not have many problems with your session, although of course Murphy's Law applies to the online classroom as well!

In many ways, preparing for a live online class is very similar to setting up for a face-to-face class.

You prepare your notes, double-check the logistics, identify the target audience and find out about the learners.

You arrive at your training room early to arrange the room and check the equipment; you check that your slides are displaying correctly on the projector and the builds are working as you had designed them; and you ensure that you have all the course materials and logistics required for the course.

Once you are ready, you go into the reception area and spend some time socialising with the learners to find out as much as you can about their background knowledge of the subject as well as what they want to achieve by the end of the course.

It's much the same with a live online course, except that you will not be physically meeting your learners, and obviously the method of delivering the session will be different.

In this session, we will discuss:

- How to get to know your audience and prepare your content to match their goals

- Preparing a Learner Guide

- Preparing the Facilitator's Session Plan

- Setting up your online classroom

- Conducting rehearsals

- How to prepare your learners for the session

Getting to know your audience

As experienced trainers, I'm sure you understand the absolute value of knowing your audience before you run the session. Having this information prior to the session enables you to tailor your session, if necessary, to ensure that it is pitched at the right level and covers what they need.

Back in the days when I was a classroom trainer, on course days I would rarely know who would be in the class and why they were attending. I'd have a list of names and companies, but no specifics on their learning objectives or needs. So the first goal of the day was to meet as many of them as I could before they came into the classroom. I was looking for any information about them which would enable me to adapt my sessions on the fly, so that they could relate the learning to their job.

When the course started, I'd ask each one to introduce themself and de-clare what they were most interested in learning that day. It was useful to gather that information, but I really wished for a way to know these details before the class started. It would have been so much easier to create an appropriate job-related example if I had had time to prepare beforehand.

In the world of online classrooms, of course, even though you probably won't know your learners either, you can plan ahead prior to the session. So your first task in preparing your sessions is to obtain the information you need to know about your learners well in advance. If necessary, you can then adapt the content to their knowledge, experience, and what they are aiming to get out of the session. Most importantly, you can discover how they will be applying what they learn when they return to their job.

So let's consider what vital information we need to gather from our learn-ers prior to adapting the content to meet their objectives. Here are some examples of the types of question you may like to use for your sessions—you can adapt the list to meet your own requirements.

- What is your job function?

- What experience do you have of using web conferencing soft-ware?

- Have you attended or presented online classroom sessions be-fore?

- Which web conferencing software have you used (if any)?

- What do you want to be able to do after attending the course?

- How often will you be using your new skills?

- What concerns do you have about the course?

All of this information can be collected through the e-mail that you send to the learners in advance of the session. Alternatively, you could use an online survey tool, like SurveyMonkey, to gather the information.

But make sure you give your learners a deadline for returning the information, and ensure that the deadline gives you enough time to make any necessary amendments to your content.

A word of advice here: tailoring content for the online class environment can take 3-4 times longer than for a face-to-face class—so you need to factor that into your schedule when you are planning your session.

Having acquired the necessary information from your learners, you can start to prepare the Learner Guide.

Preparing the Learner Guide

Let's turn our attention now to creating a Learner Guide. The Learner Guide is a reference document for learners, which contains all the basic information they need for successful attendance at the session. The Learner Guide is their 'bible', and they will want to refer to it throughout the session (or sessions if it is a multi-session course).

The Learner Guide should include everything a learner will need before, during and after the session and, importantly, details of where to find information, help and advice. A well- designed Learner Guide can often be a critical success factor in an online classroom event, and your efforts will be rewarded, as you will be able to use it over and over again to good effect.

When you create a Learner Guide, it's useful to think like a learner. As a learner, what would you like to know before the session starts? Here's a list of items you may wish to include in your Learner Guide:

- Course description, objectives and schedule

- Technical set-up and requirements—what equipment they will need, how to log in, how to set up their audio, and so on

- Contact information for the trainer and technical support

- Disaster recovery—what to do when things go wrong (connectivity issues, etc)

- Participation Ground Rules

- Schedule of live sessions and assignments (pre- and in-course work assignments)

- Web conference software screenshots, with illustrations of how to log on, and how to use the response facilities (Chat area, emoticons, and audio set up wizard)

- How to use the Learning Management System for uploading work and downloading assignments and other support materials, such as reading materials, videos, podcasts or quizzes, and so on

- Dates and times of pre-course check sessions—to ensure that the course starts off with no hitches, it's a good idea to hold a couple of 'Welcome to the Course' sessions to check that the learners can log on correctly and can set up their audio. This can save quite a bit of course time as everyone will arrive at the first session knowing that they are set up and ready to go right from the start.

Ensure learners receive their Guide well in advance of the course start date—preferably one to two weeks beforehand. It's best to convert documents to PDF to ensure that all learners have the same page numbers as you to refer to, irrespective of their own printer settings. This enables you to refer to a specific page number which will be the same for each learner.

Preparing your Session Plan

All sessions should be supported by a Session Plan, which is the blueprint of the session structure, topics and outcomes, and when and where you will be incorporating interactivity exercises. So your first task is to carefully structure the topics for the session.

Building a Storyboard for your Session Plan

Probably because live online learning has evolved from e-Learning, many people use a Storyboard to map out their session. The storyboard has its roots in the film industry and was first developed by Walt Disney in the early 1930s for one of his early cartoons, *The Three Little Pigs*. It was designed as a visual guide to the cartoon, and is basically a list of graphics displayed in a linear sequence for visualising a film. The storyboard concept was taken up by the e-learning industry for laying out screenshots for the early CBT systems and is still used by many instructional designers today.

In our live online sessions we use the storyboard concept to map out our sessions. It is a document that contains the content of the session in a linear structure which provides the 'cues' for what happens in the session. It ensures that the content and technical considerations are met in the right sequence to guide the facilitator and co-facilitator through the session. If you have ever worked backstage on a play you will be familiar with the script document which contains cues for actors' entrances and exits, as well as cues and instructions for the sound and lighting engineers.

In their book, *The New Virtual Classroom*, Ruth Colvin Clark and Ann Kwinn provide a template for the storyboard they use. It is very comprehensive, but I have seen others, which have objectives and learning styles for each topic too, but this is somewhat of an overkill in terms of what we are trying to do here. What is needed is a clear; a concise grid layout which takes you through, in sequence, what the key learning points are, what slide you should be showing on screen, what facilities you will need to deliver that segment, roughly how much time you have allocated to that segment, and what you need to be preparing for when the next segment arrives.

After producing many live online classes, I have developed my own storyboard which contains only what I consider to be the most important and necessary items. What you include in your storyboard is really up to you, but I encourage you to take a basic one and adapt it so that you are comfortable with it. Don't get bogged down with all the extraneous information that serves no purpose when you are facilitating. When you are live online you want something clear, simple and, importantly, easy to use and update.

There is a good little pocketbook for starting storyboards called 'Moleskine Storyboard Pocket Notebook', which you may find useful. You can find the details in the Resources section.

Let's take a look at the one I use. It contains just 5 columns: Time, Talk, Screen, Interaction, and Prepare.

Time	Talk (Key Point)	Screen	Interaction	Prepare
2	Need to use minimal text on the slides (less than 6 words per key learning point)	13		Get ready for Whiteboard 4 – annotation rights need to be enabled
4	Q. How could we cut down the number of words on this slide?	14	Learners enter responses on the Whiteboard using text tool – ensure colours are readable (not yellow!)	Give annotation rights. Whiteboard 4
10	Enter your responses on Whiteboard Discuss responses		Whiteboard 4 Discussions (draw out key points and reaffirm	Take annotation rights away. Open microphones At end of discussion mute microphones
15	Use of text on presentation slides	15		Load Poll 5.3
18	Different types of font – Sans Serif, Serif	15.1	Show examples of different fonts (Arial & Garamond)	

Let's discuss what goes in each column: Time, Talk, Screen, Interaction, Prepare.

- **Time**: In this column, enter the number of minutes you expect the segment to take in normal circumstances. For example, the first Key Point (The need for minimal text on the slide) is '2' showing me that I should not take longer than 2 minutes to introduce myself.

- **Talk**: This is the list of key learning points that I will be explaining—note that this is not a full script just the prompt of the Key Learning Point you need to discuss.

- **Screen**: This is the graphic file reference that I will be displaying on the screen. In my example, I am showing Slide 13 on the first part, followed by 14, then 15, and so on. If a slide has a build I would denote this as 15.1, 15.2, and so on, showing the builds on slide 15.

- **Interaction**: This is the interaction I will be conducting—such as questions, polls, whiteboard, microphone, and so on. This column is extremely useful in highlighting to me if I am not using enough interactions in the session and expecting learners to sit through too much talking!

- **Prepare**: This column is the technical 'to do' list. It identifies what item needs to be ready next—for example, start Application Share, Load Poll 5.3, assign whiteboard annotation rights to learners, and so on. This column would be the one that your co-facilitator would carry out, if you had one with you.

So a good storyboard/session plan is your guide for the whole session. It will keep the session on track and will ensure that all the important interactions are carried out at the right time. It also serves as a useful reference for your co-facilitator—if you should be fortunate enough to have one! You can download a copy of my Storyboard Template from my blog at *www.virtualclassroomtrainer.com*. Feel free to use it and/or amend it to suit—I would be pleased to receive your templates to see how you have adapted them to suit your sessions.

Setting up your online classroom

Prior to the session, there is a lot of work to do to set up your classroom. Firstly, there is the technical set-up to carry out. Secondly, you need to conduct a rehearsal to check that everything is set up and working correctly and, finally, you will need to prepare the learners so that they can log on and enter your classroom with minimal disruption. Let's go through these three steps now.

The technical set-up

The technical set-up comprises all the tasks you need to carry out using the web conferencing system. There are a lot of things to do and, if you are new to the live online classroom, I would recommend that you prepare a checklist so that you can tick off all the tasks one by one to ensure that you have covered everything. Here are the technical tasks that you'll need to carry out.

Registration

It's vitally important that your learners encounter minimal problems when they log into the system, so you need to test out the log-in procedure for learners. You can do this by creating a dummy learner and logging in on your 'learner' computer. I often say 'put yourself in the learner's shoes' and this is a good example. So log in as a learner using the information you sent them to make sure that everything is working as it should— the user experience should be as flawless as it can possibly be.

Connectivity

Connectivity issues are the main reason why things go wrong with live online learning events. It can, and often does, put people off the environment completely if this happens, especially if someone is logging on for the first time—so you must do everything you can to eliminate possible connectivity issues well in advance of the session running.

There are three main ways to prevent connection issues during your event. You can take care of two of them during your set-up, and you can advise learners about the third in your communications with them before the event.

- **First, test everything!** While you have plenty of time to trouble-shoot and make any necessary adjustments, test everything you are likely to want to do during the session. Be sure to open all files and turn on all the features you will be using in the event. Test out any videos to ensure they run correctly and download any documents that you will be providing to your learners at the end of the session.

- **Second, check your Internet connection is working effectively.** You can dramatically improve your connection to the Internet by presenting from a corporate LAN connection rather than from a wireless connection. If you are working from a wireless connection, then change it. Use an Ethernet cable connected to the router and your computer—but ensure that you disable the wireless connection on your computer otherwise you will still be connected through the wireless connection. I discovered that this is what I was doing when I first hard-wired the connection a couple of years ago. It is a simple error to make.

- **Third, optimise your computer resources.** Before any practice session or actual event, reboot your computer. Then close (not just minimise) all applications that you don't need, for instance, e-mail, Skype, background running programs, Internet Messenger, and so on. You will only need a browser and any applications that you will use if you are conducting an Application Share. Remember to tell your learners to do the same in your Learner Guide, and reinforce the message when they first join the session.

With regard to using different web browsers, I have found that Firefox causes me the least number of issues, so I always use that one.

Audio options

On most web conferencing systems, you can use VOIP and conference call facilities. With VOIP, your learners can talk and hear over your Internet connection. Some systems also allow the learners to listen and speak using a telephone. Usually you would use VOIP but, if you or your learners have problems with the audio, you may like to set up the event such that learners can use the telephone for hearing your voice while they watch the screen as normal. Note that the Teleconferencing option can be quite expensive if you have several learners—so check with your web conferencing system vendor as to the costs of providing the dial-in telephone facility.

Software and services

A key part of your preparation is to make sure you have control of the web conferencing system and the services you will be depending on. There are two items to check during your set-up:

- **Plug-ins.** Some web conferencing systems require learners to download plug-ins on their computer. If this is the case with your software (for example WebEx, Elluminate, Centra), then ensure that this task is carried out and explained—both in your Learner Guide and when you get learners to log on prior to the session. Additionally, most web conferencing systems require a small download to the presenters. So, remember to check with your IT department that this will not cause any firewall problems.

- **Preparing for Application Sharing.** To be able to share applications with your learners, you will need to have that application running on your computer when you run the session. You will need to open the application and minimise it so that it is ready for use during the session. It is possible to load it on the fly of course, but it will introduce some 'dead air time' whilst it's loading—so is not recommended. Remember that Application Sharing is resource hungry so double check that you have no other programs running, and remember to close it down when you have finished with it.

Setting up your session

At least a day before your event, you should ensure that your session is set up ready to receive your learners. This includes creating and loading all your Polls, creating your agenda, setting and configuring your break-out rooms, and converting and uploading your content. Note that, with WebEx, this is not possible before the session, so you will have to do all of this on the day itself. In this instance, you will need to prepare the session at least an hour before it is due to start.

Converting and uploading your content

It's likely that your presentation content will have been created in Power-Point, Keynote or Prezi, and possibly other software applications as well. You will need to convert this content to a format that your web conferencing software can read. Converting the files also reduces the file size, allowing the file to display on the screen more quickly.

Each web conferencing system handles presentation files slightly differently. In some systems PowerPoint files lose some functionality when they are converted. This particularly applies to animations, builds and transitions. WebEx and Adobe Connect handle slide builds fine—you simply upload the files to the system. Regarding the file format to upload, I have found WebEx's UCF add-in to PowerPoint the most fail-safe way to do that. If you are using another web conferencing system, check that it can handle slide builds and conversion automatically, else you may be caught out.

Remember that you will also need to upload your Reception Slides, which should be showing when learners are logged on and waiting for the session to start. These 'holding' slides could be:

- Title of presentation and the presenter/facilitator

- Session start and end times

- Invitation for learners to introduce themselves in the text Chat area

- Screenshots of how learners can use Chat, Emoticons, and importantly, the Audio Set Up Wizard

- Photographs and biographies of presenters

- Reminders to close all background programs and switch off any nearby phones

Show your Reception slides as a slideshow as people are logging on.

Speaker rehearsals

The second major area of production set-up involves co-ordinating with another speaker, such as your co-facilitator or perhaps a guest speaker.

If you are using another presenter or co-facilitator, it is important to hold at least one rehearsal a day or so well before the date of the session.

Conducting rehearsals

Your objective here is to build confidence in using the web conferencing system with your content, and in running through how the session will work from a production point of view. I recommend that you always re-cord rehearsals for later playback so that you and the other presenters can review how the session went and see if there are any points that could be improved.

For those speakers who have had plenty of experience of presenting online, the Speaker Rehearsals should not take too long. You will simply need to get them to run through their presentation using all of the facilities they need for their session. Obviously, you will need to spend a little time on rehearsing things like who is going to do what and when—note these points down on your session plan. You will also need to check their audio connection and that the quality is acceptable.

Rehearsing with inexperienced speakers
For those who aren't experienced at speaking online and/or using the web conferencing software, you have more work to do inasmuch that some presentation skills coaching will be required for this different me-dium. As we have explained, classroom-only skills are not enough in the online classroom.

Rehearsing yourself
If you are going to be the facilitator of the session, then the task is a lot easier as you obviously know the content of your session well and are familiar with the web conferencing system. However, all online classroom trainers always need practice. In fact, any professional in any profession should never stop rehearsing.

So run through your session a few times to rehearse the session from start to close—and amend anything in the content that you feel would improve it.

It is always very useful to run a full rehearsal with invited guests to act as learners for your rehearsal sessions.

A few minutes of planning and preparation should eliminate many potential problems and give your sessions, presenters, and materials a more polished look and feel—and that will lead to a more successful and rewarding session.

Preparing your learners

Do you really need to prepare learners? Without doubt, yes you do.

It's really important to have learners and speakers install and test the software they need, and their audio connections, well before the session is due to start. This is always where the most problems occur in online sessions—so it's best to sort any connection problems in advance of the session day.

In your communications to your learners, schedule some times when the room will be open for them to log in and test out their connections with you. These preparation sessions are invaluable and will ensure that you eliminate connection problems before the session proper, but importantly will give your learners chance to get used to the web conferencing system interface by using the emoticons and other facilities.

During these sessions learners can:

- Get a brief demonstration of the software interface

- Experiment with the basic features such as buttons to indicate status; ticks and crosses; emoticons; hands-up; and so on. They can also practise using the Chat tool—show them how to send messages to the group, to presenters and to specific individuals.

- Confirm that software installation was successful. If they are unable to join the session, ask them to contact you by phone or Skype so that you can establish whether they have carried out the set-up correctly or whether perhaps they may be experiencing a firewall problem. And, most importantly, confirm and ensure that all of these checks are taking place on the computer they will be using, and that the location is the same one they will be using for the sessions. It is of no value to carry out all of these tests at the learner's workplace if they plan to attend the session from home!

- And finally, check that they are receiving audio and that the quality is good. A note of warning here: it is important that learners use a headset and do not use their laptop's microphone and speakers, as these cause off-putting echoes in the facilitator's headset.

The more prepared you are for your online session delivery, the more relaxed you will be during your session, and the more enjoyable and effective it will be.

The more prepared you are, the more relaxed you will be

By being properly prepared you will have real confidence in your web conferencing system set-up, your knowledge of the content, and your expertise in using the web conferencing software.

So, don't overlook the importance of your preparation. Build in plenty of time to prepare fully—and double-check everything—every time you run your sessions. The more effort you put into the preparation of your online sessions, the more successful they will be.

6

Communicating in the online classroom

In this chapter, we will be looking at the techniques of communicating with your learners in the online classroom. As the online environment is primarily an audio/visual one, we need to concentrate on enhancing these skills—skills which are much more important because of the remoteness of the learners.

In this chapter we shall cover:

- Using your voice effectively

- Posing effective questions

- Gauging learner participation

- Using the web conferencing system's response features for communicating

- Some best practice guidelines for communicating effectively

90% of a trainer's credibility comes from their physical presence

In a traditional face-to-face classroom, 90% of the trainer's credibility comes from his physical presence. Being the focus of attention, our learners are constantly watching us and providing us with vital feedback via their eye contact and body language. So, in the online classroom, how do you create that same credibility and keep people engaged when you have no physical presence?

The online classroom is a very different medium from the face-to-face classroom, with vastly different rules and considerations. You obviously can't give a nod of reassurance, a smile of approval, or even a frown of disapproval to your learners. You no longer have the advantages of eye contact and body language. So you have to rely solely on the subtle cues you receive from your learners over the Internet.

In the online classroom, your voice, the learner's response from the web conferencing facilities, and your visual aids are your only means of communicating, so it is essential that you use all of them effectively.

Using your voice effectively

In the online classroom environment, your voice is your most essential instructional tool. Firstly, and most importantly, you must ensure that you have the best possible audio quality, as this can have a tremendous impact on how learners perceive the quality of the event overall. If the sound quality is poor—choppy, signals dropping, delays, echoes, and so on—it will turn learners off immediately and will start the session off with negativity.

So the importance of having the best possible quality microphone/ headset that you can afford cannot be understated. I recommend using a USB headset rather than one that connects to the computer by the line-in sockets. This provides a better quality of sound. Additionally, for good audio quality, you will need a fast Internet connection. As an online facilitator, you will need to have fast upload speeds as well as fast download speeds—you can check your connection speeds at www.speedtest.net.

Apart from the quality of the audio signal, using your voice effectively and your microphone correctly, are important techniques to acquire. A boring, slow, monotone voice will quickly create boredom and disinterest in your learners. Remember school, college or university? And those long, boring one-way lectures?

Have you ever listened to an inspiring speaker—someone like Steve Jobs, Elliot Masie, Bob Mosher, Nancy Duarte, Elliott Masie or Sir Ken Robinson? All of these speakers are inspiring for a couple of reasons:

- They are passionate about their subject

- They put that passion in their voice and it transmits directly to you

- They have pace, tone and inflection in their voice

- They are 'conversational' with a nice little added spice of humour mixed in

- They draw you in to the conversation by making what they are talking about relate to you and your circumstances

One of the best ways to learn how to project your voice, making it interesting to listen to, is to listen to a radio broadcaster. Spend some time listening to the radio to see how radio broadcasters have mastered the art of using their voice in an interesting and conversational way. Most radio stations have presenters that are interesting to listen to and make you feel that they are talking to you across the desk—not over the airwaves.

When we speak in the online classroom we have many similarities with radio broadcasters—we are both isolated by distance from our audience and, just like them, we cannot see, hear or interact with our audience as we would in normal face-to-face conversation.

When you are online, the pace at which you speak is vitally important. Too fast and the audience will not get what you say; too slow and they'll be quickly switching on to their Twitter or email accounts. When you are speaking online you need to speak more slowly than you normally would in a face-to-face conversation. But be careful it does not get too slow. Actually, the pace you use should depend on the culture of your learners. In the US, for example, they talk much faster than we do in the UK. So, if you are training in the US, keep it pacey but not too fast!

If your learners' first language is not English, then you will need to talk more slowly, and try to cut out words, clichés and colloquialisms that they would not understand—or would perhaps misinterpret or take literally (bite the bullet, more ways to skin a cat, bat out of hell, axe to grind, no use crying over spilt milk, and so on).

Here are some other tips for using your voice effectively:

- **Ensure that the microphone is at the right distance from your mouth**. If you are using a headset microphone keep the microphone slightly below your mouth. If you are using a stand-alone microphone, then 4-5 inches is close enough. A 'pop shield' will stop those awful 'pops' when you say the letter 'p' and 'hisses' when you say the letter 's'. And remember that you don't need to shout! Your microphone amplifies the sound—so talk at a normal level, as you would in a face-to-face conversation.

- **Vary your intonations**. Nobody likes to listen to a monotonous voice that drones on and on, even when there are things to look at on the screen. Remember that your voice is the star of the show, and it is crucial that you make it as interesting as possible. Remember it's not about making your voice black and white; it's about creating light and shade.

- **Use a conversational tone**. Talk to your learners as though you were talking to them face-to-face, so use 'your' and 'my' and their names, and keep it informal, conversational and friendly.

  For example, *"How would explain that Richard?"*, *"Laura, could you elaborate on that point for us please?"*

- **Be positive — and use some humour**. If you are sending out signals of anxiety or nervousness, then your learners will detect them. So you need to talk with authority and be positive at all times. It's good to be informal and friendly, so try to inject a little humour now and again. Balance is important though—so do not overdo the humour. When you use a little bit of humour, you won't hear your audience laughing (or groaning) so you need to imagine it. As in any training situation, be very selective about the humour you employ, however. While it can break the ice or lighten the mood, take care that you do not offend anyone — it's very easy to do, so stay clear of any subjects that are likely to cause offence.

- **Smile and use hand gestures**. Although this may sound odd, your learners will 'see them' through the way they alter your intonations in your voice. Although they cannot see you, using natural hand gestures as you speak will improve your intonation and delivery. I sometimes get some odd looks when people pass by my office seeing me gesturing at my laptop screen!

- **Be careful about sounding too scripted**. Unlike in the face-to-face classroom, you can get away with reading scripts in certain parts of your presentation, but be careful. If your delivery sounds too scripted, you may lose your learners' attention. Change your intonations and pace, and make sure you emphasise appropriate words and phrases. Also, if your eyes are on the script and not on the screen, you may miss important feedback from your learners.

- **Be careful about leaving your microphone live.** When you are typing in Chat, your audience will hear it. So remember to 'Mute' your microphone when you are not talking—but don't forget to 'Unmute' it when you start talking again!

- **Don't talk for too long**. Your learners' attention is difficult to capture, and even more difficult to keep. Break up your sessions with frequent interactions, but make them meaningful and in context with what you are teaching. As a general rule of thumb, if you have been speaking for more than 5 minutes, you've been speaking too long.

- **Don't overload learners with instructions**. Don't overload your learners with too many instructions at once. This is especially true for smaller groups. New learners have a difficult time retaining instructions for a lot of tasks—remember Cognitive Load in a previous chapter?

- **Watch the coughs and sneezes**! A tip here that I learned early in my experience as an online presenter—if you feel a cough or sneeze coming on, mute your microphone! Coughing, hiccuping or sneezing with your microphone live is a real 'no-no'!

To sum up, communicating in the online classroom takes on more significance and importance when you are broadcasting. As opposed to the classroom, your learners cannot see you and so your voice is their contact with you. Practise hard to get this skill right. It takes everyone many hours of practice so, whenever you can, practise speaking with a microphone. It's a good idea to record yourself whilst you are practising so that you can replay it to see and hear what went well and what went not so well. Today we have many gadgets that enable us to record our voice—I used my iPhone when I was practising, but there are many gadgets and even software (like Audacity) to help you.

Although no-one likes the sound of their own voice, you will soon hear improvement in your voice quality after listening to yourself a few times. As your confidence grows, it will become second nature to you. Who knows, you may even get a job on the radio or TV one day!

Using questions to communicate

Questioning techniques are one of the most powerful ways to communicate to your audience and are vital in learning. As an experienced trainer, I'm sure that you've mastered this art.

Most experienced trainers use questioning a great deal in talking to classes and groups, as well as when talking to individual learners. Questions are, of course, used in both verbal and written form, but here we'll focus on the trainer asking questions verbally. Many educational experts, including many experienced and effective trainers, consider verbal questioning to be one of the trainer's most potent tools.

There is a crucial advantage in using the questioning approach, and that is that the knowledge gained in this way is transferable.

Most people would agree that the questioning approach is more interesting for learners—they are actively involved rather than passively listening.

Additionally, the style of questioning will stimulate the learner's curiosity: "What ground rules would I like to have in the session?" Moreover, learners are made to think and reason in a questioning-style lesson: "What are Ground Rules for and why should we have them?".

The emphasis in a questioning-style lesson focuses on 'understanding' rather than simply 'knowing'. In a trainer talk-style lesson, the learners are simply told what they have to know; they are not encouraged to understand it, and are less likely to remember it.

As a result of the questioning, learners' own assumptions and prior knowledge are challenged and corrected. For example, before the lesson some learners did not know what Ground Rules were, what they were for, what the advantages of having them were, and so on; but, in the course of the lesson, they found out by thinking about what Ground Rules were, why they were necessary, and thought through which rules they would like to have in their lesson, and why.

There is another distinct advantage of using questioning as a teaching technique—learner motivation. Nothing motivates quite as much as the glow of satisfaction that the learner feels when she answers a question correctly and immediately gets warm praise from the trainer.

In summary, the advantages of questioning as a teaching method are that it:

- ensures that the learning is built on prior learning in a constructivist way

- produces transferable learning

- gives instant feedback to the trainer and learners on whether learning is taking place

- ensures that the lesson moves at the learner's pace

- is an active and interesting activity for learners

- gives the learner practice in using the recently acquired ideas and vocabulary the trainer has been teaching

- uncovers incorrect ideas and assumptions

- is motivational, as it gives learners a chance to demonstrate their success in learning

- offers, in a one-to-one question, the chance for the trainer to diagnose the difficulty a confused learner might be having

- allows the facilitator to evaluate learning

- encourages the development of high-level thinking skills

Questioning technique in the online classroom

How should we use questioning in the online classroom? A good questioning technique should encourage all learners in the session to think. You must avoid creating an 'I'm trying to catch you out' atmosphere, and you must give learners a chance to receive some positive feedback, which will demonstrate a success for them.

After posing a question, pause for a while; most of the learners should then be trying to think about their answer. When you have allowed a reasonable 'thinking time' choose someone to provide an answer. If you nominate someone to answer before posing the question, the rest of the learners will be mentally switched off. The longer you pause, the more thinking the learners do, and the longer their answers will be when they come.

Encourage responses to questions by asking simple ones first, especially with a new group of learners. Without going overboard, show you are grateful for their responses, and always praise correct answers.

How should you deal with incorrect responses?

Do not, under any circumstances, dismiss the answer as 'incorrect'. If a response is incorrect, simply say that you would like them to rethink their answer—perhaps you could put the question in another way to get the learners on the right track.

The technique of leading learners through the reasoning stage can also be used if they are unable to answer a question at all. Let's look at an example. In our scenario, a driving instructor is questioning Dan, our learner driver, about a driving error Dan made earlier in the lesson.

Instructor: *"You started signalling too early just then Dan. Say you wanted to turn right, when should you start signalling?"*

Learner: (Dan thinks)

Instructor: *"Can you signal right too early Dan?"*

Learner: *"I'm not sure. I suppose so."*

Instructor: *"What would happen if you signal right a mile before the junction in the city centre?"*

Learner: *"Other drivers would think you're turning right before you really were."*

Instructor: *"That's right, so when should you start signalling if there are lots of junctions about?"*

Learner: *"Just after the junction before?"*

Instructor: *"That's right. Well done."*

What can we learn from the driving instructor's technique?

The learner's confidence is boosted by the praise and smile from the instructor and, importantly, a potentially negative experience for the learner is turned into a positive one.

You may not have asked the same questions; that doesn't matter, as long as the questions you ask help the learner's think out the reasoning for themselves.

Distributing questions

When questioning during a session, try to distribute the questions as widely and evenly as possible. It's all too easy to ignore the quiet learners in the online classroom when you can't see your audience; so make sure you include everyone. In the face-to-face classroom environment, it's easy to identify reticent learners by noticing eye contact and body language cues. But this isn't possible in the online classroom, and so you must keep a tally on those who are seemingly 'sitting in the background', responding slowly when you are asking for responses, and not contributing. I always keep a sheet of paper by my keyboard to do this.

In the first session of the IITT's *Certified Online Learning Facilitator* course, when learners will not know each other, we use a great technique which involves pairing learners and getting them to interview each other using Direct Chat. We then bring the learners back together and ask one of the pair to explain what they have found out about their partner. This enables each learner to converse with someone they may not know and gets them to use questioning by interviewing their 'partner'. This immediately increases their confidence and so increases their responsiveness to future questions. It is a multi-purpose icebreaker that I recommend to you.

Varying the types of question you use

We know that there are two basic types of question—open and closed. Let's look at how we deal with them.

Closed questions are those normally answered with either a single word (yes/no) or a short phrase. The benefit of closed questions is that they:

- Give you *facts*

- Are easy to answer

- Are quick to answer

- Keep control of the conversation with the questioner

But closed questions do not necessarily check that learning has taken place.

Open questions are much more valuable for learning as they require a more detailed response and require the learners to think and reason. *"Nicki, where could we make improvements to our process for logging customer calls?"*

Open questions make learners think, and tell the trainer much more about what learners have learnt. By contrast, closed questions usually require little thought. They provide low diagnostic power—that is, the trainer cannot know for certain that a correct answer means that successful learning has taken place.

Questioning levels

Some questions simply require learners to recall facts. For example, *"When was the Great Fire of London?"* Such questions certainly have their uses—such as reinforcing earlier learning, practising recall, pointing to the most important facts in the topic and informing the trainer of what learners can and cannot remember.

However, there is much more to learning than remembering. Even the most experienced trainers would acknowledge that most examination syllabuses award less than half their marks for the recall of facts. The majority of marks are awarded for higher order skills, such as the ability to comprehend and apply the concepts and principles associated with the course of study. Factual recall questions do not by themselves develop understanding, and they do not encourage learners to apply their knowledge, let alone practise the higher order thinking skills.

Facts are often soon forgotten—the dates of Henry VIII's reign, for example, will soon be forgotten unless recalled from time to time. Open questioning techniques require the learner to use and develop their higher order thinking skills and, in a culture such as ours, the importance of these skills can hardly be overstated; once developed, such skills can be applied to any field of human endeavour.

For the majority, who find little direct use for most of the factual knowledge gained during their education, these skills are the main benefit of their many years in school or college. These precious thinking skills can only be developed by the effective use of questioning. Their use also ensures understanding of the content.

Questioning does not come naturally to many novice trainers, who are accustomed to thinking in terms of answers rather than questions. As a result, many novice trainers find it very difficult to sustain a lengthy bout of questioning, requiring as it does the ability to think on your feet in order to field an unexpected answer and turn it into the next productive question.

It is advisable to prepare in advance the questions you will use in the session, especially the thought-provoking ones. However, it won't be long before you are able to think up questions on the spot.

To summarise, questioning is of paramount importance. It would be impossible to develop genuine understanding, or other higher order mental skills, without it. It teaches learners to think for themselves, and produces high-quality, transferable learning. It enables learners to practise using the concepts and principles that are being taught, and provides trainers with feedback on whether learning is taking place and ensures that they don't 'lose' the learners.

Learners tend to find questioning an active and enjoyable activity, especially as answering correctly gives them confidence and the feeling of achievement. Even learners who are not chosen to answer the question will gain in confidence if they are able to think of correct answers for themselves. This feeling of confidence and success, along with the praise and approval which should accompany it, fuels motivation.

Here are some important lessons for using questioning in the online classroom:

- **Use questions throughout your session — at least every 3-5 minutes.** To encourage participation, you should use questions often throughout your session. Try to vary the response mechanisms you use, however—don't just keep on using Polls for example. Make sure you make use of Chat, the Whiteboard as well, and give learners the microphone so that they can explain their responses.

- **Call on learners by name**. I always try to use learners' names when responding to them. This increases the sense of community within the group. Whilst we're on the topic of calling learners by name, I want to highlight where I differ from what is written in some of the books about facilitating in the online classroom. Most of the textbooks say that by pouncing on learners to get them to answer a question you are encouraging them to pay more attention. To some extent, this may be true. However, I am not particularly enamoured by this—especially in the early stages of a session, and particularly when they are a new group. My view is that by pouncing on learners you are in danger of making some feel apprehensive and uncomfortable, and you can certainly make them feel embarrassed if, say, you ask the question that they cannot answer. Remember, unlike the face-to-face trainer, we do not have the benefit of body language to enable us to judge how someone might feel or respond. My advice is: wherever possible give them notice (and time to think) before you call on someone: *"James, I will call on you next to ask your views on..."*. So respect your learners; don't embarrass them.

- **Ask learners to raise their hands when they are ready**. Rather than pouncing on someone when you have posed a question to the group, ask your learners to use the Raise Hand icon to signify they are ready (or have completed the task you set). By using this technique you can see who is switched on, by the speed at which they respond. But you do need to be aware of anyone who is slow to respond as they may be having some difficulties. If everyone has 'raised their hand' except one particular learner, don't wait too long for them to do so. You could check in private Chat whether they need more explanation. This technique provides you with valuable 'online body language' feedback.

- **Tell your learners how to perform a task**. There are some natural ways to get feedback in the face-to-face classroom. For example, when a trainer asks if anyone has a question, they look around the room to judge the body language of the learners. In an online classroom, what should learners do when asked if there are any questions? Should they respond by clicking 'yes', 'raising a hand', or putting their reply in the Chat area? If they have no questions, is the proper response to do nothing or to click on the 'no' button? Similarly, if you say "*Click yes when you're ready to move on*", how should learners respond if they are not ready to move on? Should they click 'no', 'raise their hands', or do nothing? It can be confusing for the learner, can't it? So remember, whenever you ask learners to do something, tell them exactly how you want them to respond to you.

- **Have a bank of questions prepared**. It's useful to have a text file of questions prepared for your session and open ready to use. For ease, just cut and paste them into Chat rather than typing them into Chat on the fly. It's unprofessional to hold up learners whilst you take time to type in your questions.

Gauging participation — online body language

Being able to gauge whether the learners are 'with you' is, of course, difficult when you can't see them. Because learners are not under the watchful eye of the trainer, the danger is that they will multi-task—even though they have agreed not to as part of the Ground Rules for the session. Of course, whilst they are attending to emails or posting on Twitter, they are not paying attention to the lesson.

So how big a problem is learner multi-tasking during online events? Recent research by the 1080 Group, a firm of consultants in the US, found that over 90% of learners admit to multi-tasking during the session. Although the competition for learners' attention is strong, and may appear daunting for the trainer, there are many ways to keep track of the learners' activities.

Reading learners' engagement cues

One of the most important tasks for the online trainer is to keep an eye on learners' cues—just as any trainer would in the classroom. But, being remote from your learners, you will need to tune into some different cues.

You will need to tune into some different cues

Here is a list of some of the ways you can gauge 'online body language':

- **Note how long it takes for the group to provide feedback and answer Polls**. Those taking much longer than you expect are probably not paying close attention or are struggling with the content. So keep an eye on the feedback you are receiving from the Response tools.

- **Are they responding quickly?** Another cue to gauging learners' attention can often be judged by the pace at which they respond. You can glean some rich cues about learner comprehension during the administration of a quick group Poll—for instance, who is slow to respond, who waits to see how others reply before offering their own opinion, and who switches the vote a few times before settling on an answer? Having said that, bear in mind that it takes a few seconds to think—and then some more time for them to type a response in the Chat. But if you notice that someone is regularly slow to respond, it should give you a clue as to their level of engagement or comprehension of the topic.

- **Are they tuned-in?** If your learners are unresponsive or slow to volunteer, you might have to force class participation. For example, you could have all learners raise their hands before you ask a question, then call on them in the order their hands were raised. You have to mix it up occasionally, perhaps by calling on them in random order. The less predictable you are, the more your learners will need to stay tuned in. So keep them on their toes.

- **Do they use emoticons regularly?** Another useful form of feedback from your learners is to get them to use emoticons regularly. The trainer should actively make the use of emoticons a welcome and routine part of live online interactions. Reward learners for using them in some way. Specifically asking learners to submit a Green Tick to express comprehension, or a Raised Hand to request additional guidance, is a highly effective way to take the virtual pulse of the group and quickly gauge the atmosphere in the room. Some learners, or trainers for that matter, may refrain from using these because they consider them unprofessional, or are simply not accustomed to using them. So get learners into the habit of clicking on emoticons right from the start of your session. And remember to do so yourself too! One way of rewarding learners is to give them Applause for a good answer, or click on the Light Bulb icon (if your web conferencing software has one) when someone has brought a good idea or explanation to the group. I am sure you can think of many useful little ways of using them. These real-time emoticon responses can provide the encouragement and confidence every learner needs—it's the equivalent of a nod from you that says "very good, keep going", so the student knows whether they're doing well or whether they should ask for more guidance.

Communicating using the response facilities

Let's turn our attention now to how you can use some of the web conferencing system tools to communicate with learners in order to engage them and obtain responses.

Chat

Chat exercises can be a great outlet for the excess energy typical of kinaesthetic learners. You can use Chat to capture the results of a brainstorming exercise, or suggest ways to relate the topic you are teaching to their job, for example. Using Chat for responses to questions is a really good way to break up larger topics in your session.

Here is a nice technique we use in our sessions—the Type & Hold technique. Sometimes you may want to ask for feedback from all of the learners but need to ensure that they are really thinking about their answer. In our Type & Hold we ask everyone to enter a response in Chat—but not to press Send until instructed to do so. When they are ready, get them to Raise their Hands. When everyone is ready, count down to their pressing the Send button. Using the Chat to accomplish this gets everyone engaged and it's a bit of fun everyone likes.

Here are some useful tips for using the Chat area:

- **Select the right recipients**. Remember to explain to learners how to select the correct target recipient in Chat. They should be careful to select 'All Participants' in the Send To line as the message then goes to all presenters and learners. Often learners choose 'All Attendees' and this just goes to the other learners— so the message is not seen by the facilitator or other presenters. I fail to see why there is an 'All Attendees' option, but perhaps I am missing something.

- **Provide time boundaries**. It is a good idea to give specific time limits to Chat exercises and let learners know when they have, say, 15 seconds left. Obviously, you would only do this on an exercise where perhaps they would spend some time working out a solution to a problem. You would not do this in an ordinary question-answer sequence.

- **Allow learners to reflect on the other responses**. It is important for learners to have time to compare and contrast their own responses with everyone else's. Encourage this by saying: "*I'd like everyone to look at Jill's response, and then take 30 seconds to write down what you think has led her to make that decision. Please respond in the Chat area.*"

Polling

The Polling feature provides buttons that the learners click to indicate their selection from a list of options. Some advantages of polling include the speed and ease of administering questions, the opportunity for all learners to respond, and the ability to display responses, either by individual learners—and/or in an aggregated format. Polls are easy to set up, but make sure you set up your polls in advance of the session. Do not create them 'on the fly'.

- **Use Polls throughout your session**. Typically, the trainer prepares the Polls ahead of the lesson and activates the Poll at the appropriate time in the session. Try to spread them out—Polls are frequently only used at the beginning of a session to gather feedback from the learners, but you should be mixing up your interactions throughout the session.

- **Use Poll placeholder slides**. I have often seen presenters leave a previous slide on screen whilst conducting a Poll. It looks sloppy and unprofessional so don't do it! It is best to create a Poll Placeholder slide with the question as the title; this focuses the learner's mind only on your Poll.

- **Broadcast results only when everyone has responded**. The facilitator can choose to let everyone see all of the responses to the Poll in the learners' information window or they can keep the individual responses hidden from the learners if greater anonymity is desired.

- **Provide a summary of the results**. When the results of a Poll are broadcast, it's a good opportunity for starting a discussion to draw in the learners and get them working and collaborating. Perhaps you could take the opportunity to ask a learner why they chose a particular option. You could then extend the discussion by asking other learners to provide their views. Apart from using Polls to gain instant feedback, think of Polls as a way to start a group discussion.

Whiteboard

The Whiteboard is one of the most collaborative tools in a classroom, especially for visual learners. It allows for instant visual communication and invites everyone to participate. Kinaesthetic learners also appreciate the ability to interact physically with the tool itself, because it helps keep their attention focused.

The Whiteboard typically contains some combination of annotation tools enabling every learner to type or draw on the Whiteboard. The following annotation tools are available in most web conferencing systems: pencil, eraser, text, colour, lines and various shapes, providing learners with the facility to be creative if required.

The reason why I particularly favour using the Whiteboard often is that it allows all of your learners use the Whiteboard at the same time. The same is true of Chat, of course, but the Whiteboard provides additional ways for learners to communicate other than just via text—for example, learners can draw pictures, highlight something on the screen, and so on—and so it provides a much more creative way of communicating.

Here are some tips on how to use the Whiteboard:

- **Plan exercises**. Prepare your exercises well in advance of the session. For example, you may have to prepare a grid with boxes beforehand to allow each learner to add comments in 'their box'. Another nice touch is to put each learner's photo in 'their box'. People like having their own 'space' in which to work.

- **Encourage creativity**. Instead of instructing learners to type their responses, encourage them to draw pictures, for example: "D*raw how you are feeling today*"; "*Draw a picture of your favourite hobby.*"

- **Involve everyone**. If only a few of your learners are writing ideas on the whiteboard, encourage the reluctant ones to do likewise. Perhaps you could ask them to comment on the ideas or to interpret the pictures.

- **Play some games**. With a bit of creative thinking, you can draw up your own online game. For example, have learners draw missing parts of a diagram, complete a crossword puzzle, do a word search or play a quiz-style game. This is a great way to reinforce content, energise your audience, and have some fun at the same time.

Whiteboards are really useful for collaboration and learners always enjoy using them. And, once again, they are a really good way to bring in discussions—so don't limit yourself to only using the Whiteboard for writing or drawing.

Emoticons/Response Icons

We have already mentioned that the trainer should actively make Emoticons a routine part of live online interactions. Specifically asking learners to submit a Green Tick to express comprehension, or a Raised Hand to request additional guidance, is a highly effective way to take the virtual pulse of the group and quickly gauge the atmosphere in the room. Get your learners into the habit of clicking on emoticons. And remember to set the example yourself too.

Webcams/Live Video

Most web conferencing systems provide a facility for a live video feed from the trainer's webcam, which is typically shown in a small window on the screen. Seeing a live video feed of the trainer enables learners to see the trainer live—creating a classroom-like connection.

But it should be used very sparingly. Using it throughout the session—apart from hogging the bandwidth and slowing the connection—is a distraction for learners whose eyes will naturally be drawn to movement from your webcam, rather than concentrating on the slides. So, at most, I would recommend using your webcam at the very start of your presentation, and then perhaps at the end in the Q&A session.

A short live video introduction can help to reduce the feeling of remoteness that learners may feel, so use it by all means. Here are a few points to bear in mind:

- **Look directly into the webcam when you talk**. This establishes that important eye contact. However, it is a difficult technique to learn—I suggest that you keep a post-it note on your screen to remind you to look at the webcam all the time it is live.

- **Use your normal hand gestures whilst on camera**. When you are speaking 'on camera' use the hand gestures that you would naturally when speaking to someone across your desk—nodding, gesturing, smiling, etc.

- **Make sure your webcam quality is good**. Take care to ensure that your webcam picture quality is good. You will need to set up your webcam prior to the session, checking both the lighting and the backlighting.

- **Finally, be careful what you show on camera**. Before you show your webcam live to the audience double check that the camera does not pick up something in the background you do not want broadcast!

So that concludes how to use the many tools that the web conferencing system provides for communicating with learners.

In summary

Remember that you will not have perfect classes all the time. If you go with the flow and embrace the experience, your expertise and enthusiasm will put your learners at ease, thereby creating an environment conducive to learning. So keep your voice tone relaxed, informal and conversational, but vary it often to keep that broadcaster high energy level up.

Trainers should be masters of communicating with their learners. But in the live online environment there are new skills and techniques to learn and master. After plenty of practice, you can be a master of communicating in the online classroom too.

In the next chapter we shall be exploring how to manage your session.

7

Managing and facilitating your session

So, you've done your planning, prepared your content, produced your slides and supplementary content; you've also contacted your learners, found out about them and what their objectives are, and ensured they know how to connect to the session and log in. Now it's time to start facilitating your session!

Just as with any classroom course, there are many things you can do in the 'opening' phase to make your event a success. In this chapter, we are going to concentrate on performing a professional opening of your session, and then we'll explore and discuss best practice facilitation techniques. This is based on lessons learned after conducting many events online. There are several checklists to ensure that we cover all the bases.

In particular, we shall be covering:

- Ensuring a professional opening

- Dealing with connectivity issues

- Handling latecomers

- Dealing with technology that lets you down

- Dealing with questions

- Conducting Application Sharing

- Conducting Web Browse

- Conducting Breakout Rooms

- Using media

Opening your session

One of the most important things you can do when running live online events is to ensure that the way you open your session is professional and grabs the learners' attention from the start. If you do not get them at this stage, you will struggle to get your learners back. A professional opening will set the tone for the rest of the event; therefore, it's vital that you handle this well.

So let's look at how to go about opening your session professionally.

Log into your room an hour before your session starts

Firstly, try to log onto your web conferencing system an hour before the session start time. This sounds like an awfully long time before the session starts—it's not; you will need that time to do last-minute checks and collect yourself ready for the first learners to arrive.

Having this time available will allow you to make any last-minute adjustments to the room and enable you to have a quick run-through to ensure that the slides and other content are looking and working correctly.

I usually find it best to block any early arrivals coming into the room (most systems allow you to do this) until I am completely sure that everything is ready for the session to start. You don't want learners watching you fiddling about on the screen.

Start background music

Once you have checked everything thoroughly, you can open up the room for those eager learners who have logged on early. At that point, open up the room and play some background music. I know that some people are not that fussed about having music playing in course rooms whilst they are waiting but, online, I think it's extremely valuable for you and your learners.

I find that the benefit of having the music playing is two-fold:

- Firstly, being able to hear the music confirms to learners that their audio is working fine, rather than their having to wait for the session to start to find out that they can't hear anything. I have logged into many Webinars and assumed that I have logged in correctly—but always, in the back of my mind, I wondered whether the session was taking place, as I could hear no sound at all.

- Secondly, it confirms to people logging on that the session is actually taking place. On a few occasions I have attended sessions where I could hear no sound and was unable to see the list of names of other participants; so I was left wondering whether I was the only one attending, or even whether the event was taking place at all. This is also compounded when you are attending an event from a different country from your own as there may be time zone issues. Having music playing in the background, being able to see the session title and start time on the opening slide, and seeing a list of participants and Chat being used, eliminates those fears.

Of course, with small-group events, you would ideally fade out the music when you have a few learners logged in so that you can open their microphones and get them talking and discussing what they are hoping to take away from the session. This 'socialising' is extremely important in the early stages of the event and mirrors what they would be doing naturally in a physical classroom. What you are doing is making the technology transparent and enabling your learners to become comfortable with the virtual environment.

Background music has some real benefits — but you need to get a PRS licence

Finally, on the subject of music, you need to consider that if you are broadcasting music then you may need a licence from the Performing Rights Society.

Start Reception slideshow

With around 30 minutes to go to start time I start the Reception slide show and keep an eye out for the first learners to enter the room. By now you should have carried out all of your pre-session tasks, so it's a good time to ensure that you have a glass of water and a notebook nearby, and have switched your mobile to silent. Additionally, it's a good idea have a final refresh of your Session Plan whilst you are waiting for your learners to arrive.

Welcome learners personally

I always welcome every learner as soon as they have logged into the room, but I do not necessarily use a microphone at this stage. Why is this? When learners log in, they can see the slides and hear the music, so they know that they have connected successfully. The slides will also show them how to use the Chat and check their audio using the audio wizard. I do not think that you should pounce on learners immediately, so a nice welcoming message in Chat gives them the opportunity to respond without any pressure.

Remember that many people are new to the live online environment and may feel a little apprehensive. Pouncing on them to speak over the microphone is not a good idea.

With 15 minutes to go

With 15 minutes to start time, the countdown is now in full swing. Hopefully learners would have logged in with time to spare and will be using Chat to socialise with the rest of the group.

Here is how I use the countdown time before we start the session proper.

- **Get everyone settled in**: The idea is, in these first few minutes, to get everybody settled in and comfortable, fired up for the start—and ready to learn.

- **Make announcements**: I usually make an announcement over the microphone, welcoming everyone as a group. I encourage them to use the Chat to introduce themselves to me and the other learners. I ask them to let us know where they are attending the session from, their job function, and what they are looking forward to in the session ahead. Another often-used 'icebreaker' is where you display a map on screen and ask everyone to click on the map the location where they are attending from, using the Annotation Tools. This is usually a good way to start people chatting.

- **Check that everyone's microphone is working correctly**: Now is a good time to go round the group to open the microphones and check that everyone's is working correctly. If there are any audio connection problems you have time to fix them before the session starts.

- **Confirm start time**: This is also a good time to confirm the session start time, end time and the goals and outcomes for the session.

- **Set Ground Rules**: I also reiterate that learners should disable programs running in the background—including email, Instant Messenger, Twitter etc, as well as reminding them to put their phones on silent.

With at least 5 minutes to go

- **Announce the speaker**: I make a further announcement and a further welcome, and encourage anyone who has not entered their details into the Chat to do so.

  If I am hosting or co-facilitating the session, I also announce the speaker and provide a brief background on them, and let everyone know that we will be starting on time. I also reaffirm that I expect learners to ensure that their e-mail and phone are switched off so that they can concentrate on the lesson without distraction.

Dealing with connectivity issues

Learners having problems connecting to the session is always going to be one of the first things you will have to deal with before the session starts. There are basically two ways to handle this: firstly, ask them to carry out the audio check using the Audio Wizard if they haven't already done so.

The problem is usually that they have not selected their headset for the microphone and speakers. If this doesn't cure the problem, then advise them to log out of the session and log in again using the original link you gave them in the invitation email.

Remember that you should have already ensured, in the pre-preparation stage, that they were able to log in successfully, so if they are using the same computer, the problems are likely to be one of those highlighted.

Handling latecomers

One of the most frequently asked questions I receive is how should you handle latecomers on a session. This is a dilemma that you will have to deal with quite frequently as many people leave it to the last minute to log on, only to find that they have a problem connecting.

So, as the facilitator, with learners waiting and ready to start the session, what should you do if one or more of your delegates is unable to log on? Should you hold up the session whilst the latecomers sort their problems out? Or should you continue with the session even though you have some learners missing?

You could start without them, wait another five minutes, or wait until they eventually arrive. My advice is: don't wait for them longer than that, and only doing so after checking with the rest of the group that they are happy to wait.

When the latecomers do eventually log in, you should acknowledge them and briefly explain where you are up to in the session—but be brief so as not to hold up those that were on time any further. If you have a co-facilitator, it is best to get them to perform that task using private Chat.

On with the show!

Firstly, remember to start recording the session—it's so easy to forget it when you are just about to get started on the content. I have found that the best time to start the recording is just prior to switching over from your Reception slides to your main session slides. Of course, you could start it whenever you like, but check with your web conferencing vendor that you have the facility to edit the recordings. This is an important facility as you can delete unwanted pre- and post-session material.

I recommend that you tell your learners that the session is being recorded and confirm that it will only be available to the learners who have attended the session.

If learners think it may be shown in the public domain it could make them hesitant to respond so well. Imagine how you would feel in a face-to-face course if you knew that it was being recorded. In that circumstance, you would probably be more hesitant to come forward with answers or opinions as freely as you would if it wasn't being recorded. So in the interest of your learners, put them at ease about the recording right away.

Introductions

You probably already introduced yourself when you first started speaking, but it is important to introduce yourself properly to your learners to signal that the session is formally starting. Display a slide with your photograph and some information about your credentials for teaching the session. If you have a co-facilitator, then you should do the same for them too.

Ground Rules

The next task is to re-state the session Ground Rules. These rules set the tone for the session—that is, what you expect from the learners and what they can expect from you. Your learners should be familiar with them by now as they will have been issued to them previously in the Learner Guide, but to state them again will reinforce the message.

Here are a few of the most common ground rules—you can design your own of course.

- **Turn off email and phones—and clear other distractions away.** In today's connected world it is all too tempting to get distracted. The danger is that if a learner stops paying attention to answer the phone, read their Tweets, pick up some paperwork, or answer an instant message, they will lose track of what is going on in the session. The facilitator will not know that the learner is not paying attention and so they won't be able to engage him successfully. I always ask learners to only have their web browser running on their computer and to disable any programs that may be running in the background. You obviously can't make them do it, but, if you explain why it's important, the majority will—and of course you have the 'Attention Meter' that highlights which learners are not paying attention!

- **Participate and prepare to be called on**. The online environment lends itself to lots of interaction. So this rule is important as it keeps the learners on their toes, especially if they think they may be called on to answer a question or to give their views. By letting your learners know right from the outset that they will be called on throughout the session, it sets the tone that the session is a working event—no 'lean-back and listen' training here folks!

- **Raise your hand if you have a question or comment**. Let your learners know that they are welcome to ask questions at any time. When a learner clicks the Raise Hand icon on their screen, an indicator appears next to their name on your screen. This is an extremely useful facility as obviously you can't see whether anyone wants to ask a question. Additionally, if more than one learner 'raises their hand' the system puts them in the order that the learners clicked the icon, so you can answer the question in the order asked without writing it all down.

- **Be patient waiting for a response to your question or chat message**. Obviously, whilst you are facilitating the session you are concentrating mainly on that and can often miss raised hands or questions in Chat, especially if you are not fortunate enough to have a co-facilitator. So ask your learners to be patient and trust that they will always receive a response to their query; however, they may have to wait until an appropriate break in proceedings.

- **Notifying absence**. If you have to leave your desk for any reason, please click on the Step Away button and when you return click on the Step In button. One of the emoticons on everyone's screen is a Coffee Cup (in Adobe Connect it's a 'Step Away/Step In' icon). Tell the learners that, should they need to step away from their computer for any reason, they need to click on this icon to signify they are not there temporarily. This is important, because you must know when you can call on someone, and when to wait for someone to respond in a poll. If the learner has his Coffee Cup icon on, you will know not to wait for a response from them.

Using the learner response tools

Now that the warm-up and introductions are done, it's time to get the learners used to the software interface before they focus on the session content proper.

Your first task is to get the learners working interactively right at the start of the session. For a new group, I always provide them with a brief overview of the learner response tools, concentrating on how they interact both with me and their fellow learners.

So take them through the facilities and get them to use them—say, by asking for a Green Tick if they can hear you clearly. One of the better ways I have seen of doing this is to play the 'Simon Says' game by using the emoticons. This always goes down well and provides some light-hearted fun and banter among the learners.

I also get them all to enter into Chat a response to a social question, like *"What's one thing that most people wouldn't know about you?"* or *"What is the weather doing where you are?"* This always provides some interesting comments from learners and quickly establishes the community spirit within the group. But make sure you keep it conversational and informal—use their names as much as you can.

In a small group, I then concentrate on getting them to speak in the microphone, by asking them questions such as: *"What part of the session are you looking forward to most?"* or *"What part of the session are you apprehensive about?"* This gets the likely apprehension about using the microphone out of the way early and makes them feel 'more connected' with the group and comfortable. You know what it is like if you have never spoken in public before—it is a daunting experience for many people. So try to get that out of the way as early as you can.

Note that you can design your own methods, of course, but try to follow the structure of getting learners comfortable with the interface and interacting with you and their fellow learners as soon as possible.

This prepares your learners to be tuned-in and ready to learn—they should not have any apprehension about attending and should now be concentrating on you and what you have to say. You have their attention—don't let them get away until the end of the session!

Disaster strikes and the trainer loses connection

Much as I hope it never happens, Mr Murphy will undoubtedly raise his head at some stage during your online trainer career and, mid-way through your session, your Internet connection will fail—and you will have lost connection with your learners!

So, where is your classroom full of learners? Are they out there some-where wondering what's going on or have they all lost connection and are sitting at their desks not knowing what they should do? Should they phone you or wait to be called?

The answer is that they are all still connected together in the online class and are probably happily chatting away on their microphones (if you left them open) or conversing in Chat discussing what they should do.

Connection problems will strike sometime — so be prepared!

So, what can we do to prepare our learners for any lost connections? The answer is that, both in your Learner Guide and at the start of your ses-sion, you should have provided instructions outlining what they should do if you lose connection. You could give them an exercise to do in Chat— it's a good idea to ask for a volunteer learner to take on the role of facilitator until you get back online. Or you could simply tell them that if you (as the facilitator) do lose connection you will be back within 5 minutes and, if this is not the case, you will contact them all to reschedule the session.

If you have a co-facilitator with you, the web conferencing system will automatically hand over control of the session to them, so obviously they will take over until you get back online.

Tips for facilitating your session

Here is a list of tips and techniques that you will find useful as a new facilitator in the online classroom.

When should I take questions? Another question I'm regularly asked is: "When is it best to take learners' questions?" Should they ask questions during the session? Or should they save their questions until the Q&A session at the end?

- **Take questions when best for the learners**. I have read many articles on facilitating online learning sessions and there seems to be no definitive consensus of opinion. I believe it really depends on how you think learners learn best. Although it can be off-putting to have questions fired at you throughout your session, causing you to keep stopping to answer them, I think that this is the best method. So you should answer questions when they are being asked because, obviously, the learner is confused, does not understand, or has a query on a point. However, you must not spend too long answering questions such that it develops into a long Q&A session.

- **Keep it on topic**. There is always a danger that questions and answers can quickly go off topic. If a learner starts drifting off into other areas you should bring them back on topic by a gentle instruction, such as, *"Debbie, this is a good discussion but I will take it up in the Q&A session at the end"*.

  It also serves a gentle reminder to the other learners to stay on topic.

Answering questions: As experienced trainers, I'm sure you are aware of the reasons for, and benefits of, asking questions of your learners. We covered this earlier, but it is vital that you get this right—so let's just re-cap:

- **Ask lots of questions**: One sure fire way to obtain feedback from your learners is to ask for it, so ensure your sessions contain lots of questions throughout. Web conferencing systems provide several ways for you to ask questions, and several ways for learners to respond to them. It's up to you and the instructional designer to determine how best to craft multiple choice, multiple answer, yes/no, and open-ended questions, and how best to instruct learners to use these tools.

- **Vary question types**: Don't rely on using the same methods to get feedback as this soon becomes boring. So mix it up a bit by using different question types to get response from learners, such as leading questions, review questions and asking for opinions.

Conducting software demonstrations

For those who will be conducting software demonstrations in their sessions, you will no doubt be making a lot of use of the Application Sharing facility to demonstrate software products.

One of the major benefits of the online classroom environment is the ease with which applications can be demonstrated using the Application Share tool. So let's spend some time looking at facilitating this aspect.

- **Use the actual application**. For conducting software demonstrations, it is always best to use the actual application itself rather than putting up a series of static screenshots on the slides. So you will need to get the application running on your desktop before you start your session.

- **Application Sharing needs practice.** It takes a while for the novice facilitator to get used to be able to use Application Sharing professionally, and you'll need a lot of practice before you can feel comfortable using it. Please don't 'wing it'! Practise it thoroughly.

- **Explain how to use the 'Floating Windows' (in WebEx)**. You will need to explain to learners how to open up their Chat and Participant panels so they can communicate with you. As the facilitator, you will obviously need to open them up too—but make sure you do not open them over the main screen or your learners will suffer from 'cross hatching' over their screens (see below).

- **Beware of the dreaded Cross-Hatch!** When conducting Application Sharing you must be aware of the Cross-Hatch problem which occurs when you open another panel whilst working with the application. If you open another panel on top of what you are showing on your screen, it will show on the learners' screens as a cross- hatch and is a real distraction for learners. Having your second (learner) computer to see what the learners see is a real bonus when using Application Sharing.

- **Be aware of time lag**. When using resource-hungry facilities like Application Sharing, you should be aware of any time lag between what the facilitator's screen displays and when it appears on the learner's screen. So, when demonstrating applications, keep your eye on your second computer screen to check that the application is showing on the learner's screen before you start your demonstration.

- **Disable background programs**. Finally, Application Sharing takes a lot of bandwidth, so it is especially vital that everyone does not have any background programs running.

Besides having the ability to display the live application on your computer for everyone to follow your demonstration, Application Sharing allows you to pass control of the application running on your computer over to a learner. In this way the learner is able to use the application as though it were residing on his own computer. As you'll no doubt agree, one of the best ways for learners to learn a new application or functionality is by letting them use the application itself.

Can you think of some ways your organisation could use this facility? It has tremendous possibilities—take IT support for example. The IT support person could obtain control of the user's computer firstly to correct a problem on the computer and, secondly, to walk the user through how to solve the particular problem such that they truly understand how to correct the problem should it arrive in the future.

Back to a live online session, and an important point if you plan to use Application Sharing in your sessions. The only downside of using Application Sharing is that, when you hand over control to a learner, it is only really engaging one learner—the others are passively watching what is going on. So ensure that you pass the control of the application around and let all learners have a turn at practising what you are showing them.

Conducting a Web Browse

The facility to share your Web Browser is a really useful one for online classes—you can show all of the learners a website which is synchronised to what is showing on your screen. In this way, you can ensure that all learners are watching exactly what you are showing and explaining. This would be useful for new recruits to show them the company intranet, for example.

Whilst using Web Browse, there are a couple of points just to be aware of. You should have the website you are going to show running in your browser before your session starts so that the transition from your slides to the browser is as seamless as possible. In this way, as long as your web browser is already pre-loaded—or saved as a quick link—you can jump right to it without stopping on your browser's default home page with everyone waiting whilst you type in the web address. Be aware, though, that if you plan to type in the website link, it may display your browser history—so it's best to clear it before your session as it may be showing some confidential web links.

Conducting Web Content in Page

This is similar to conducting a Web Browse, but it has a major difference: whereas in Web Browse everyone is synchronised to your web browser, in Web Content in Page they are not synchronised. This means that learners could go off on their own exploring whichever links they choose—so you have no control over what sites they are seeing.

This facility is aimed at enabling learners to explore the web on their own. It would be useful for an exercise where you want them to conduct some research on a subject, for example.

Using Breakout Rooms

The facility to set up and run breakout sessions in your online sessions is probably the most useful facility provided by web conferencing systems. They are the best way to get your learners collaborating and learning together in groups. The bonus is that they are easy to set up and so you can run them often in your sessions—and I have found that learners like the breakout sessions best.

You run Breakout Rooms exactly as you would when you have syndicate room sessions on your classroom courses—although obviously you do not have to keep walking up and down the corridor to do so!

In the Breakout Room the learners have their own facilities— microphones, Chat and Learners' Panels, Whiteboard and so on. You will need to appoint a group leader, who is in control of the microphones and annotation tools for the Whiteboard, just as a presenter does in the main room.

Facilitating a Breakout Room session is tricky to learn at first and takes some practice. But do not let this restrict your use of the facility. I have found that Breakout Rooms are the best way to engage your learners— so try to use them often.

Bear in mind, though, that they do eat up lots of session time, which means that you can quickly fall behind schedule. So plan Breakout Rooms into your sessions allowing enough time for the group work to be completed.

Here are some useful tips for facilitating Breakout Rooms:

- **Monitor rooms**. Make sure that you visit the Breakout Rooms often to check on each group's progress and answer any questions and queries they may have. It is easy to do this and I would advise you to make yourself available from time to time—but make sure you go into the rooms too often. Let them work, discover and learn together rather than 'holding their hands' during Breakout Room exercises. Remember, people learn from making mistakes and discovering things for themselves, so give them plenty of opportunities to do so.

Set time limits. Another important point to remember when facilitating Breakout Rooms is to set a time limit for the exercises. Before you place learners into Breakout Rooms, post the aim of the exercise and the outcomes you are expecting on the Whiteboard. Additionally, it's important that you let them know how much time you have allocated to the exercise, so put that on the Whiteboard too. When it's almost time to bring the groups back from their Breakout Rooms, give them a two- minute warning that the time is nearly up. Remind them also to ensure that the group leader saves the Whiteboard to their own computer so that the file can be uploaded into the main room when you carry out the debriefing exercise.

Using Hands-on Labs

WebEx Training Centre has a facility called Hands-On Labs, which allows each participant attending a WebEx session to be connected to a PC. This 'Virtual PC' environment can be used by the facilitator to give learners the opportunity to run Windows and applications installed on the PC as though they were local to their machines.

This facility provides a tremendous benefit of live online learning as it enables learners to carry out exercises and use the programs on a remote computer—dedicated to them—so that they can learn and practice using the application in a safe environment. The benefit is that every learner can be working, rather than the 'one at a time' practice provided by Application Sharing.

Showing video clips

The facility to transmit video in your sessions is invaluable for learning. Although I was not really convinced that the bandwidth was there for it to work successfully, recent advances to the video facilities in WebEx and Adobe Connect have made a tremendous leap forward.

Showing video is invaluable in your sessions — but you need to keep them short

Before the upgrades to video facilities (Spring 2011), the problem was that when you 'show' the video, it first has to download on each learner's computer. Depending on their connection and bandwidth these times can vary and you could be waiting a while before the video is ready to show.

However, after some trials just prior to this book being published, the upgraded video facilities seem to have solved the problem and short video is now a viable option for your online classroom sessions.

Another way of showing video is to upload a video clip you want to show to a video streaming site like YouTube or Vimeo. You could use the Web Browse facility and show the YouTube video this way. This does work, but the problem we frequently come across is that many organisations' firewalls block video streaming sites.

So there are some considerations for you to think about before you go headlong into inserting video clips in your sessions:

- **Videos are bandwidth-hungry**. Videos take up a lot of bandwidth, so it is always wise to check thoroughly during your rehearsals. There is nothing worse than watching a choppy video that keeps stopping every couple of seconds. It can definitely hinder learning rather than enhance it.

- **Check software for types of files the system can handle**: Most web conferencing systems can handle showing multimedia files extremely well. But you may need to check your software to see what file types you can use. For example, in Adobe Connect you need to upload Flash video files (flv). Additionally, you should test any files on your second computer to check that they will run smoothly on the learners' computers.

- **Embed media clips**: Another thing to bear in mind about using multimedia clips is that it is usually best not to embed the media into your PowerPoint slide—it's much better to load the file into your web conferencing system for quicker replay.

- **Many organisations block access to video sites**. A frequent problem we encounter on our certification courses is that many organisations block access to external video sites for security reasons. So well before you run your session you will definitely need to check with your learners that their organisation will grant access to the particular video streaming site that you intend to use in your session.

- **Keep your videos short**. There are undoubtedly great advantages in showing videos in your sessions but there are timing considerations to bear in mind. You need to ensure that the video clip is of a reasonable duration—keep them less than 5 minutes or so if you can. Besides the bandwidth issue, you will not want to spend too long watching videos in your session as your learners should be doing things, not passively watching. If you want them to watch a longer video, say as part of an assignment, it would be much better to make that an offline assignment rather than wasting the interactivity and 'learning by doing' that the live online classroom provides.

We have now explored facilitating your session and, in particular, have covered opening your session professionally, handling latecomers, dealing with technology when it goes wrong, handling questions, and using the various facilities that the web conferencing software provides.

In the next chapter we will look at some tips and techniques on how to maximise the engagement of your learners.

8

Maximising learner engagement

Throughout the book so far we have been learning that delivering online classroom sessions that are highly interactive and engaging is the single most important thing you can do to achieve a successful event. In this chapter, we are going to focus on how to really get your learners engaged in your sessions.

Some of the content we have covered already, but here we will provide best practice tips and techniques that will enable you to grab your learners' attention right from the start—and keep it right to the end.

We will cover:

- Ensuring learners are engaged throughout the session—rules of engagement

- Making your sessions learner-centred

- Applying your questioning skills to optimise learner engagement

- Utilising the response facilities to engage learners

Rules of engagement

I'm sure you've heard the face-to-face classroom session after lunch referred to as 'the graveyard shift' or, as I read the other day, the 'Teflon
Hour'—as nothing ever sticks. We all know it's a challenge at that time of
day to keep our learners' attention and to engage them in the class.

In the online classroom, the problem of engaging learners is even more
pronounced. There are so many things going on to distract us these
days—emails, Twitter, Facebook, instant messaging, online games on
our phones, phone calls—the list is endless, and ever growing. Learners
are often shielded from these interruptions and distractions in the face-to-
face classroom setting as the trainer is with them in the room. However,
when the learner is seated in front of a computer, attending a live online
session—either at work or at home—those distractions are simply not
easy to ignore.

Although the facilitator will ask learners to switch off these distractors, we
have to rely on the goodwill of each learner to do so. Whilst you would
hope that everyone follows your advice, it is unlikely that everyone will.
There will always be someone who will leave their emails or mobile
phone on. We have to accept that. So here is the dilemma when running
an online session:

- Learners are not under the watchful eye of the facilitator

- Learners are usually in the office at their desk with the usual distractions around them—phones ringing, general office noise, interruptions from colleagues, and so on

- Learners new to live online learning do not realise that they should be 'participating' rather than sitting back prepared to be lectured at

It is therefore vital that we design and facilitate the event such that the learners have to be engaged and participating in the class. The skill required by the live online facilitator to completely absorb learners into the session through frequent interactions is of paramount importance.

Let's look at some ways that we can do this:

Make it matter

One of the best ways to get learners engaged right at the start of the session is to 'make it matter' for them—it's the 'What's in it for me?' syndrome.

So you need to help them see the benefits of attending the session, show how it will help them in their job, show how it will save them time, and so on. If it really is important to them—in other words they can see a benefit for themselves—then they will be much more likely to be engaged.

So how you can do this for your sessions? Think about one of your courses now and jot down some 'What's in it for me?' statements for the learners.

Here's an example for a course on sales training. Start off your session with a Whiteboard exercise. Ask your learners to list specific problems they face during a sales call. Discuss all of the problems with the group and let them know that you will be covering how to eliminate those issues throughout the course. As you go through the course, keep referring back to those problem issues they have highlighted and cover them off as you go.

Get their attention from the start – and keep it

It's important to capture your learners' attention as soon as they log in. Use this 'waiting time' before the session starts to talk to them and get them chatting to the other learners too.

Using the excellent 'Attention Meter' in WebEx, I have carried out a small study and have found after over 100 sessions that if you do not engage learners within 20 seconds of their logging on they will start multi-tasking. So, as soon as they log on welcome them, using Chat or the microphone, and get a conversation going: ask them questions such as "*What are you most looking forward to today?*", "*How will this session help you in your job?*", "*What do you want to be able to do after the session?*" Of course, you can ask anything—it does not have to be session- or work-related, although it should be topic-related. Here are a few more 'icebreaker' ideas:

- Share a learning-related quotation and ask for their comments

- Post an interesting statistic about the topic and ask why this may be

- Open up a poll question and ask learners to respond

- Post a map and ask them to annotate where they are attending from

- Open a Whiteboard and invite questions about the session topic

Keep it relevant

Keep the content relevant to the learners. Use stories, scenarios and examples that are relevant to their job or their organisation. For example, you could relate the current topic to a common challenge they have in the workplace. Let's say the learners come from an administration department of a hotel chain and the session is about personal security. Create the session around a scenario in the department—let's say that there has been a spate of incidents where some handbags have been stolen from the washrooms. Immediately the learners can see the 'WIIFM?' issue and will start engaging—you need to keep that engagement throughout the session. So, do everything you can to keep the content relevant to them. The more relevant the material, the easier it is for learners to stay engaged.

Encourage socialising

In the face-to-face classroom, learners naturally socialise with each other before the class begins. In the online environment they may feel isolated and remain 'hidden'. I have found that most people are reluctant to enter a Chat message until everyone else is doing so. It seems that no-one likes to be the first! So strive to create an inclusive experience by asking them to enter something in Chat, say, "*Julia what's your job role in the organisation?*" or make it non-job-specific like "*Julia, what's your favourite hobby?*" or "*Julia, how did you find logging on today?*".

Bring your session to life

Explain things through analogies, stories and scenarios, rather than just through lectures. For example, instead of going through a 4-step decision-making process, you could display a visual to match each step. This 'visualising the message' technique is a good way to engage learners and aid learning. As you build the steps, they will be intrigued as to what is coming next.

Focus on the learners

This final tip on engaging learners is the most important. Effective online facilitators always focus on the learners—not themselves. So dispense with those long introductions about you, what you have done and how wonderful you are. Remember a golden rule of training delivery: "It's not about us—it's all about the learners and their learning."

Make your sessions Learner-Centred

We learned in the Designing Content chapter to make your session learner-centred. We learned that learners must have frequent opportunities to 'construct the knowledge' through active engagement.

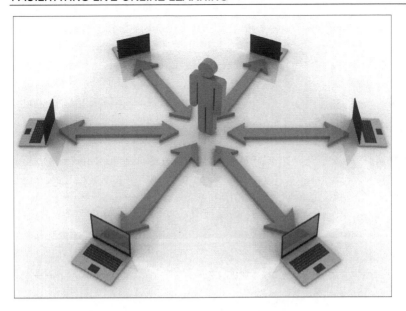

Beware of instructor focused events – the 'sponge' approach to training

Courses that are basically instructor lectures assume that learners are able to *take meaning* (or understanding) from the information provided. This is sometimes referred to as 'the sponge' approach to learning. The sponge approach—where the instructor pours out content and the learner (hopefully) absorbs it all—is doomed to failure. You are just overloading your learners' brains with information—you might as well have given them a document to read instead.

So we need to provide learning environments that put the learner at the centre of the experience—thereby providing greater opportunities for active building of new knowledge and skills—and ensure that the knowledge and skills are transferred from Working Memory to Long-term Memory.

Learner-centred environments are the best way to build knowledge and skills. One way you can increase the amount of time learners are engaged is to convert traditional didactic teaching sequences into inductive learning events. So what are inductive learning events?

In a traditional classroom training presentation, the instructor presents the content, provides examples, and then asks questions to promote understanding and address any misconceptions. This is sometimes called 'Tell and Test' training. In this scenario the facilitator is active for two thirds of the event and the learners are active for one third if they are lucky! In reality, it's probably closer to one tenth!

In inductive sessions, the percentages are reversed: the facilitator is active for one third of the event and the learners are active for two thirds. So, the facilitator provides content/examples and the learner discovers (and makes meaning of) the content and practices.

We have already covered Discovery Learning (learning by doing), but it is worth revisiting it here. Discovery Learning is a method of enquiry-based instruction and is a constructivist-based approach to learning. The method ensures that learning takes place through learners drawing on their own experiences and prior knowledge, and is a method of instruction in which learners interact with their environment by exploring.

Of course, there are some sessions that are not particularly appropriate for the inductive method, but inductive sessions are best for teaching concepts or principle-based tasks that can be illustrated with multiple examples.

Some notes on inductive events to bear in mind

- **Review examples, reflect**. Learners will need time to review the examples, reflect, and abstract the common features of the examples.

- **Inductive events take two to three times longer to facilitate**. According to Ruth Colvin Clark and Ann Kwinn's book *The New Virtual Classroom*, the increased participation required by an inductive event will take two or three times longer than the traditional approach. The payoff will be higher participation ratios, leading to greater satisfaction with the lesson and increased ownership of the content. You will need to decide which topics in your lesson should be taught inductively.

- **Identify content for inductive events**. Note that we are not advocating a complete abandonment of Tell and Test instruction.

However, one way to minimise the 'sponge' approach to learning is to identify important content in your lesson that would be best delivered via inductive learning.

Applying your questioning skills for engagement

So let's focus now on the use of questions to engage our learners. What we are concerned with is applying our questioning skills in the online environment.

Start your session with a Lead-In question

A good technique is to start your session with one or two topic Lead-In questions. This technique is designed to stimulate interest in the topic, activate learners' prior knowledge, and help focus attention on the session outcomes. For example, at the start of your session, ask a question, using a Poll, to ascertain what experience your learners have in either attending or presenting live online sessions. Note down the responses, then choose a couple of learners and ask them to elaborate.

Another use of topic Lead-In questions is to gather learners' views, on their prior knowledge of the topic, using a Whiteboard or Chat. Take a note of the responses for each learner and then ask them the same question at the end of the session.

For example, at the start of the session ask: "Rate from 1 (low) to 10 (high) how confident you feel about ... (insert the subject of your session)".

Then ask the same question at the end. If you have done your job effectively, those scores at the end should be nearer to the 10 by some degree than they were at the start of the session.

Use open and closed questions

Experienced instructors are familiar with open-ended and closed-ended questions. Open questions will certainly make learners think, reason and reflect. Get them to answer in Chat, the Whiteboard and/or over the microphone.

Give your learners time to think

The point to bear in mind when you design your course is that responses to open questions consume more session time than closed questions. Learners need time to consider their answers and articulate their ideas. In the amount of time it takes to pose and process responses to one open-ended question, three or four closed-ended question responses could have been discussed.

Of course, there are times when open-ended questions are more appropriate. For example, when an issue arises that is likely to have a variety of potential responses that cannot be readily pre-determined. Questions such as: "*Simon, please describe an experience you have had similar to the one given?*" Or "*What reasons do you have for your response?*" are classic types of open-ended question.

When you use open questions, it's best to use the Whiteboard, Chat, or preferably the microphone so that you can get the learners to elaborate on their answers and encourage discussion with the rest of the group.

Here are some useful tips in using questioning for engagement:

- **Use a combination of question types**. It is a good idea to use a combination of open and closed questioning: for example, start with a closed-ended question, perhaps using a Poll, and follow it up with an open-ended discussion of reasons for the choices each learner has made.

- **Open Questions – use Chat and Whiteboard**. As open questions mean that you are asking learners to think and provide answers which are more than selecting a yes/no or multiple-choice option, always use Chat, Whiteboard or microphone to allow learners to express themselves.

- **Closed Questions – use Polling or Response icon**. In contrast, a Poll or Response icon (tick/cross) are best suited to closed questions, which can be framed as 'yes-no' or multiple-choice options.

Be inclusive—use questions everyone can respond to

Previously we distinguished between response options, that allow everyone to respond simultaneously, and those that are more suited to a small group or an individual. For the most part, favour those facilities that permit everyone to respond together rather than those that only permit an individual response. For example, use the Polling, Chat and Whiteboard facilities to enable everyone to participate at the same time, rather than the Audio or Application Sharing options, which permit only one individual to respond at a time.

If your classes are small, the Whiteboard also offers a forum for multiple responses—learners can enter text, draw, or mark up an image displayed on the screen.

The occasional use of audio is recommended for responses to open-ended questions and elaboration on closed-ended responses. This will maintain social presence and keep learners alert because they know they could be called on at any time.

Mix it up—don't be predictable

Web conferencing systems provide excellent facilities to engage your learners, so try to use them all if they are appropriate. But the key here is to mix it up a bit so that it doesn't become predictable. Don't just rely on, say, Chat all the time for learners to provide their responses. Predictability equals boredom!

Using the web conferencing facilities for engagement

The web conferencing facilities provided in all of the major systems actually offer you more opportunities for frequent learner interactions than do most traditional classroom settings. Frequent and effective use of these response facilities is the single most important technique in achieving successful online learning events.

Let's take a look at the response facilities provided by web conferencing systems and discuss how you can use them to keep your learners engaged in the session.

Audio

One of the best ways to engage learners is to get them to speak to you and the rest of the group by using their microphones.

You can ask learners to provide verbal answers, explanations or participate in discussions. Remember though, that to allow them access to a microphone you need to give them rights to do so.

A good way to use audio for engagement is to pose a question and ask learners to click on the Raise Hand icon when they are ready to answer; then ask some of them to provide a response. Calling on learners on a regular basis will ensure that they are switched on and tuned in to the lesson. Remember to call on them by name.

Another benefit of using Audio is that it increases social presence and community spirit in the session. The social and community spirit that is naturally created in the face-to-face classroom is one of the facilitator's primary goals to achieve in the early stages of their sessions.

Chat

Chat is probably the most used facility in the online classroom. All web conferencing systems incorporate a Chat area in which the facilitator and the learners can type text statements. Each learner's name appears next to their message, allowing easy identification of the person entering the text. Chat enables the facilitator to direct the text to other speakers only, or to individual learners or all learners. The same is true (if enabled by the facilitator) for learners.

One problem that frequently occurs is when learners do not select the correct target for the Chat message in the drop-down list and frequently send messages to the presenter. This means that the other learners do not see the message, which may be a question or an answer to a question. Conversely, another problem is that they often send messages to 'All Attendees'. 'Attendees' are the learners (not the presenter or host) so, often, messages are not seen by the Presenter, even though the learner thinks they are. So always remember to explain to learners to select 'All Participants' so that everyone can see the message.

For the facilitator, the main benefit in asking for answers to be posted in Chat is that it is inclusive—everyone is involved. You can use it to set up and maintain a sense of community in the class, but its main use is to gain response from the learners.

Let's look at how Chat can be used by the Facilitator and the Learners:

- **Facilitator questions**. For the facilitator, Chat is a good option for getting answers to questions requiring brief open-ended responses. Similarly, it is useful for questions that require a brief response. For example, the facilitator can ask everyone to "*State one thing they already know about ...*".

- We use a good technique to maximise participation and thinking: we sometimes ask everyone to type in their answers, but to refrain from pressing the 'Submit' button until the facilitator says to do so. In this way, reflective learners have more time to consider their answers without being distracted, or possibly influenced by, the other learners' answers appearing in the Chat window.

- **Learner questions.** From the learner's perspective, Chat can be used to converse with other learners and/or the facilitator at any time, either publicly (to everyone) or privately (to directed people only). Obviously, it is imperative that the facilitator keeps their eye on the Chat throughout the session. A really useful way of encouraging interaction and engagement through Chat is by using the Paired Chat exercise. Let's look at how that works:

  Firstly, pair up learners to get them to interact using Chat. It's often useful to match up learners by pairing the experienced with the non-experienced, or the more collaborative with a quieter learner. Additionally, you could match them by similar industry or company.

  Next, explain how to use Private Chat: Each pair interacts using the Private Chat facility—that is, they send a direct message to their partner. Note that you will need to explain how to send a direct message and also let them know that only the Paired Partners can see the chat.

  Then give learners a time limit for the exercise. You should always provide a time limit, so tell them how long to spend on the exercise. Then bring all learners back to explain their findings.

  When the exercise has finished, ask each Pair to use the microphone to explain the results of their discussion—but remember to involve everyone.

Remember to keep an eye on the Chat panel at all times so that you can see how the learners are responding—it's a good way to gauge how engaged they are.

As I've already mentioned, this is not easy as you are concentrating on delivery, but it does get easier with practice.

Polling

The Polling facility enables the facilitator to conduct polls to gain consensus information from the learners as a group. This is a very useful way of quickly gaining the views of the learners—so, for example, you could use it at the start of a topic to see what their experience and/or knowledge is of the topic, or you could use it to regain their attention quickly in a longer session—or perhaps use it at the end of a topic to gain feedback.

The Polling facility allows the facilitator to set up the Polls before the session starts—note that you can set up Polls on the fly but this is not recommended and should be avoided.

The Poll is presented as a question with a list of 3-5 options from which learners can choose and click to select. You generally have a choice of Multiple Choice (single or multiple answer), and free text options. Typically, the facilitator activates the Polling window at the appropriate time in the session. Once the results are collected, the facilitator can choose to let everyone see all of the responses or can keep the individual responses hidden from the learners if greater anonymity is desired.

Some advantages of Polling include the speed and ease of administering questions, the opportunity for all learners to respond at the same time, and the ability to display responses, either by individual learner and/or in aggregated format.

Here are a few techniques for using Poll effectively:

- **Think carefully about your choice of options**. Polling options work best for structured interactions such as questions with three to five response options. So think carefully about your choice of options.

- **Broadcast results and summarise**. Once you have broadcast the results, provide a summary. You may like to ask a learner or two to explain their choice to the rest of the group. Discussions after polls are great for getting learners involved.

- **Using Polls as quizzes**. Apart from using Polling for gathering responses from learners about their views or experiences, Polls can be used for Quizzes or Tests. When you compile a quiz, think carefully about the answer options you provide—the idea is to make learners think. For that reason do not make the 'correct' answer too obvious and never use trick questions.

However, bear in mind that you do not have to use the Poll facility all of the time to get results from the group. For instance, you could produce a slide displaying a pie chart on which learners use the annotation tools to highlight their name on the option. Alternatively, you could use the Whiteboard by, say, drawing a grid and asking the group to enter their choice of option.

Whiteboard

The Whiteboard facility is an excellent inclusive way to engage all of your learners in group participation. Web conferencing systems allow facilitators and learners to type onto the Whiteboard and, using the annotation (mark-up) tools provided mark it with highlighters, pens, lines, boxes and symbols. This allows those visual learners to be creative with the annotation tools. Remember, you will need to provide them with mark-up rights, however.

Another excellent use of the Whiteboard is to show, say, a screenshot of an application and, using the Whiteboard's annotation tools, ask the learners to highlight where they would find, say, the Sum function on an Excel screen. But be careful using this if you have a large class; your Whiteboard may quickly become cluttered and unreadable!

Another useful feature of some web conferencing systems is the facility for the facilitator to save the Whiteboard screens for bringing back into the session or reviewing later.

We have found that the Whiteboard is the most popular facility in small group events, save for the Breakout Rooms, so use them often in your sessions to gain maximum engagement.

Response Icons/Emoticons

All web conferencing systems provide a bank of Response icons/Emoticons to enable the learner to provide feedback to the facilitator. These help to make up for some of the missing 'eye contact' that you get in the face-to-face classroom.

Learners should be encouraged to use them so that you can receive instant feedback especially to identify a learner's understanding or confusion. For example, the facilitator can say: *"Now that I've demonstrated this feature let's go on to practise. Click on the Green Tick if you are ready for practice or click the Raise Hand icon if you have a question"*.

Alternatively, if learners have been working on an exercise in a workbook, the facilitator might say: *"Now work on the exercise on the Whiteboard and when you are ready to continue click on the Raise Hand icon"*.

These simple features are really useful for instant feedback. Here are a few tips on using them:

- **Encourage learners to use them**. It's a good idea to encourage learners to use Response facilities spontaneously. If learners agree with the statement, or like an activity, or even one of your jokes, encourage them to click on the 'Applause' icon to show approval. Get learners to use them often as it will help keep them engaged. Of course, you should set an example by using them to give your learners visual feedback throughout the session.

- **Step-Away/Step-In**. One important Response icon is the use of the 'Step Away/Step-In' icon (or the Coffee Cup icon in WebEx). It is important for you that learners use the Step Away icon if they have to leave their computer for any reason; this is to ensure that you're not waiting for them to respond when they're not there. Of course, make sure they know that they need to click on the 'Step-In' icon when they return to the session.

- **Clear Response icons**. Finally, remember to clear all responses that are displaying in the Participants panel when everyone has finished responding—you can do this in WebEx by clicking on the Eraser button. If you leave responses displaying whilst you carry on with the session, learners will be distracted and will fiddle around on the screen trying to remove them themselves. Additionally, when the facilitator next asks for responses, the previous questions will still be showing. So get into the habit of 'Ask question—get responses—clear icons'.

Application sharing

Now here is a facility where live online training scores heavily over face-to-face classrooms—Application Sharing. Most online classrooms allow facilitators to share an application residing on their computer in the Application Sharing window of the learner's screen.

Managing a shared screen needs practice because in some web conferencing systems your application takes up the whole of your screen, which means you lose visual contact with your learners by not seeing the participants, Chat, and other useful panels. This is not the case with WebEx, however, as you get a small window at the bottom of your screen which allows you to re-open the panels.

The Application Sharing facility is an excellent way to demonstrate a live software application and even give your learners the chance to interact with the application from their computers.

Additionally, the facilitator can access an application on the learner's computer and can also pass control of an application to individual learners. As the learner takes control of the application, their actions and explanations are seen and heard by everyone.

Some points to consider

- **Don't fall into lecture mode**. Whilst running an Application Sharing session you can easily fall into the trap of going into boring 'lecture mode' by presenting a lengthy demonstration. So ensure that you make your demonstrations interactive—create a series of tasks for learners to allow them to practise using the application, and give them a chance to use it from their own computers.

- **Not inclusive**. The facility is excellent and has many plus points, but be aware that when you hand over control of the application to a learner, the others are still just watching. So try to devise exercises where you can pass control around to different learners.

- **Needs practice**. This facility does take some practice by the facilitator though—so ensure you are fully conversant with how your web conferencing system handles Application Share as it does differ between the different systems.

Breakout Rooms

Breakout Rooms are probably the best and most popular feature in interactive online events and I encourage you to use them as often as you can.

A number of research studies have shown conclusively that, when effectively structured and facilitated, learning in small groups can be more effective than learning on an individual basis. (*Clark & Mayer, 2003; Jonassen, Lee, Yound & Laffey, 2005*)

The use of Breakout Rooms is one of the better ways to engage your learners. Much the same as you would in your classroom, the Breakout Room facility enables you to split your group into various separate online rooms for the learners to carry out a task. After a pre-set period of time, you can then bring them back into your main room for sharing information and discussion.

As an example, structured, short, case scenarios can be discussed and responses entered on the group's Whiteboard. When everyone reconvenes in the main room, the group spokesperson can summarise the team's discussions and findings.

Managing the Breakout Rooms facility is a little tricky to master at first—so you need plenty of experimentation and practice. If you are fortunate to have a co-facilitator you can get them to handle the administration side of things (like setting up the Breakout Rooms and allocating learners to each room) while you concentrate on facilitating the groups. It is also beneficial to have a group leader in each room who is conversant with running the web conferencing system and its facilities.

Here are some guidelines to maximise success in your breakout room exercises.

- **Keep groups small and diverse**. Typically, an activity involving three to five learners in each room is just about right. You will need the group to be small enough to promote everyone's involvement yet large enough to yield different perspectives and sufficient resources to a discussion or project. There is some evidence that groups comprising learners with varied backgrounds and abilities are better for learning than are groups comprising learners with similar knowledge, industry, or departmental backgrounds.

- **Structure the breakout room activity**. Rather than giving an open-ended assignment such as: *"Discuss how you might use different media in a blended learning solution"*, provide a more focused scenario and set up a template on the Whiteboard for each group.

- **Keep the activity or discussion focused and brief**. It's best to keep your activity focused on one topic. Additionally, you should set a time limit for completion of the activity and ensure that the learners have enough time to think, discuss and formulate an outcome. Give them ample warning when the exercise time limit is coming to an end to enable the group leader to save the Whiteboard to their computer for uploading in the main room when they all reassemble.

- **Monitor small group activities**. Just as in a face-to-face classroom, the facilitator should move in and out of the breakout rooms to monitor the discussions and provide coaching as required. There is a balance to be struck here though—do not pop in and out of rooms too often as it will hamper the open discussions that should be taking place.

Maximising learner engagement is the key to successful sessions and we have looked at ways to ensure that we get that engagement at the start of our session and keep it until we sign off. Most experts agree that learners should be asked to participate at least once every 3-5 or so minutes—that's at least 12 times in a one-hour session.

But of course, you should not be governed by 'one interaction every 3-5 minutes'. Rather, you should use interactivity when you need it—it could be that you have 5 interactions in the first 2 minutes. On the other hand, do not use interactivity for the sake of it—each interaction should be meaningful, in context with the workplace, and challenging. Get that right and you will have a successful session.

In the final chapter we will be exploring how you should close your session, follow up with your learners and carry out those important performance assessments and evaluations.

Closing your session and following up

In the previous chapter we focused on how to maximise learner engagement. And so we enter into the final phases of facilitating your event—the Q&A session, closing your session, and following up with your learners to help them with their continuing development.

This part of your session is as important as the opening. The goal at the end of the session is to leave your learners energised and eager to continue learning—maybe from a follow-on session or perhaps by finding out more about the subject. From the facilitator's viewpoint you need to find out how they intend to put what they have learnt into practice at their workplace.

In this chapter, we shall be looking at:

- Handling the Q&A sequence to clear up any issues that learners may have

- Delivering a professional close to your session which leaves the learners eager to continue their development

- Assessing the performance of your learners to ensure that their learning goals have been achieved

- Assessing your own performance and how it may be improved for next time

- Following up with your learners once the session has finished

The Q&A sequence

Once you've completed the session, you should conduct a Q&A sequence to deal with questions that may have arisen throughout the session that have not yet been answered.

The best way to handle a Q&A sequence is to get learners to use the 'Raise Hand' function and then take the questions in the order asked. WebEx has a nice facility in that it attributes a number next to each raised hand, showing you the order in which the questions were asked. In that way you can answer questions in the correct order.

In the Q&A sequence, encourage your learners to use their microphone to discuss the question. This is much more valuable for the learners than simply using Chat for taking questions, as it promotes discussion between all learners rather than the 'Question-Answer', next 'Question-Answer' process that occurs when they are dealt with in Chat.

If learners prefer to enter questions in Chat, it makes it trickier for the facilitator as it's easy to miss some, especially if all the learners enter a question at the same time! If you have a co-facilitator, it's very useful if they can take charge of this aspect. Bear in mind, though, that it may take learners a while to type in their questions, so be patient! Waiting for questions to appear in Chat may seem like a long time with nothing happening but stay with it; your learners will be thinking and then typing. If more than 6-10 seconds elapse and you still have no raised hand or text in Chat, call on one of the learners and ask them if they have any questions. I have found that this more often than not gets a response and a question from someone! Once that happens, more tend to follow and soon everyone is joining in the discussion.

Here are some guidelines for conducting a professional Q&A session:

- **Encourage all learners to ask questions**. If the number of learners is reasonably small, say less than 10, you may like to call each learner directly for a question. This sometimes elicits questions that a learner was hesitant to ask but, when asked directly, it often draws them out.

- **Go back to appropriate slides**. If you need to explain a point covered previously, go back to the relevant slide. It is more helpful in terms of the learners' understanding to see the appropriate slide again—and the key learning point you were trying to put across—rather than the Q&A slide. But be careful how you do it—flipping through your slide deck looks unprofessional. Ensure you go directly to the slide in question. If you have produced your slides correctly, each one will have a title, so it should be easy to find them in the web conferencing system using the drop-down list of slides.

- **Going back with an answer**. A final tip: if you promise to go back after the session with an answer – do it. Make a note of the question, and the learner who asked it, and action it as soon after the session as you can. There is nothing worse as a learner than waiting for an important answer that doesn't arrive after it has been promised.

Remember, your job as a facilitator does not end with the session. Once the Q&A session is complete, you can then stop the Recording and go into what I call the Wrapping Up phase.

Wrapping up your session

The Wrapping Up phase is where—as in a classroom—you tidy up all the odds and ends that need attention at the end of the course.

Test and/or End-of-Session Questionnaire

At the end of the session you will probably want to conduct an end-of-session questionnaire to ensure that you have successfully conveyed the key learning points and have satisfied the learners' outcomes. You may decide to conduct an online test, or provide an end-of-session (or end-of-course) questionnaire.

If you prefer to conduct the evaluation online, you can either use the Polling facilities or create an online test using the web conferencing system (WebEx has a separate 'Test' facility) or a web-based product like SurveyMonkey, or perhaps you may have created a quiz from a program like Articulate Quizmaker. This could be carried out at the end of the session, although I believe you will get more meaningful and valuable results from conducting a questionnaire 2-4 weeks after the event.

Access to slides and supplementary material

Give your learners information on how they can download any supplementary material such as guidelines, checklists, reference material and articles. This may be via a link to your VLE or website or, as in the case of WebEx and Adobe Connect, you can enable learners to download all of the documentation from the online classroom itself—provided you had set up that facility when you prepared your room, of course.

Their Next Steps

I am a great believer in helping learners in their learning journey, and I believe it is really important to coach them in how to apply the knowledge and skills they have gained from your session and how they can continue their development. It is important to point your learners towards the next step in their development to encourage them to continue learning. A key message here is that the course, workshop or session is just the starting point.

Always give your learners follow-up learning activities

When your session is finished, let your learners know what the next step is. It may be that you point them towards the next session in the course or to a follow-on or higher-level course that they may need or be interested in. Additionally, you may like to provide a list of recommended reading, like books, blogs, articles, websites, where they can obtain further learning materials.

I recommend that you set up and manage a networking forum site so that all your past and future learners can continue networking, sharing ideas and resources, and learning from like-minded professionals. There are many free (or minimal cost) online networking sites available that provide all you will need. You could also run some follow-up sessions for all past learners—a virtual conference session with some well-known speakers, perhaps? With today's social networking facilities, you can achieve most things at little or no cost—you are only limited by your imagination (or sometimes your IT department).

Your Contact Details

Finally, let your learners know how they can contact you after the session has finished. As previously discussed, this can be via an online forum that you have set up for learners, your e-mail address, blog, and your Skype and Twitter addresses, for example.

Close down and log out professionally

You have completed your Wrapping Up and hopefully everyone is satisfied and eager to continue with their learning using the tools and facilities you have pointed them to. You now need to close down the session in the same professional and positive manner that you opened it.

The way that many webinar presenters just end a session leaves a lot to be desired. How many times have you attended a webinar or online event and, at the end of the session, the host or presenter says: *"Thanks for attending, hope to see you next time,"* and then shuts down the system leaving you in limbo? To me, it's like the trainer in the classroom saying: *"Right that's the end of the course, thanks for attending,"* and then promptly walking out of the classroom and slamming the door! Not a professional way to close a session is it?

So, at the end of your sessions, let the learners know that you will stay online for 5-10 minutes to answer any questions or help with anything they may need. Then tell those that are ready to leave exactly how to do it: *"To leave the session, click on the File Menu and choose 'Leave the session"*.

When everyone has left your classroom—and only then—you can shut down the web conferencing system.

Cleaning up your online classroom

Depending on your web conferencing system, when your session finishes you may need to clean up your room ready for your next session. The Adobe Connect system retains your room and all of its contents, even though you have logged out, which means that it is set up ready for the next time you log into the room.

However, with other systems, you will need to set up your room from scratch every time you use it—WebEx Training Centre is one such system.

Once you have exited from the system you will be given the option to save any files that you created in the session. This is a useful facility which enables you to go through the files to pick up on things that could be useful for when you look at updating your session for next time.

Let's look at the files you can save.

- **Save the Chat as a text file** so that you can have a look at it later. If there is no such option in your web conferencing software, just copy the text and paste it into a text document. Having the ability to go through your Chat file is invaluable. For example, if you ran out of time to respond to all questions during the session, you can go back and answer the questions afterwards. Additionally, by looking at the Chat 'transcript' from the session you may be able to pick up points of confusion or identify a topic that the learners were having trouble understanding. All of this information will help you to amend the session for next time.

- **Save the Whiteboards**. You can save all of the Whiteboards as individual files to your computer. Besides reviewing how they were used, you can often pick up good ideas from your learners by looking at how the Whiteboard was used. Once again, a good way to upgrade your sessions.

If your system is the permanent type (like Adobe Connect), where the content stays in the room even though you have closed it down, you will need to prepare it ready for next time you run the session:

- **Clear the Polls**. Your Polls are probably saved to your computer as you should have set them up prior to the session; so you just need to clear the Poll results to make sure they are clean for next time.

- **Delete your presentation slides**, unless you will be using the same slide deck in the next session.

- **Delete your supplementary materials**, unless you will be requiring them for the next session.

Edit and post your recording

Finally, you will need to post the recording of the session and send the link to your learners so that they have the facility to go back through the session if they need to refer to a particular point or just need to recap on a few points. Learners appreciate this facility and find it particularly valuable.

Some web conferencing systems allow you to edit the recording. You can tidy up your recording by cropping out any unwanted parts – usually at the start and end of the session. Note that not all web conferencing software has the facility to edit recordings.

Evaluating the session outcomes

Sometime after the session, say 1-2 weeks, you should conduct an evaluation. Now, when I say evaluation, I certainly do not mean filling out a 'happy sheet'. For me, they have little value.

What we must do post-session is to explore how effective the session was for the learners—did it satisfy their learning goals/needs? What worked well for them? What could be improved to help them and make their learning experience better? Did the session provide the skills they were seeking and have they used those skills back at work?

As previously stated, there are various ways to collect and evaluate the data, but for now let's just concentrate on some of the things you may like to collect your learners' views on.

When I ask learners to evaluate the session, I want to know:

- Did the session satisfy their personal objectives/learning needs?

- How did the session work for them—both technologically and educationally? If the technology was an obstacle, it's important to know that so that you can, if possible, put it right next time you run your session.

- Which topics did they get most benefit from – and were there any that were of little value to them? Quite often it's a good idea to get your learners to rank the topics in order of value to them, with short explanations if possible. You get much more from their words and feelings than a ranking number.

- How could the session be improved? Once again, try to get them to explain rather than using a rating scale.

- I also ask how they would rank their confidence in using the skills before the session and then rank it after the session. I usually provide the options of a 5-point scale, where 1 is low and 5 is high. This gives me a good perspective on the success of the session in terms of skills transfer.

- Have they started using the skills they learned and practised on the session now they are back at work? If not, find out how long until they anticipate doing so (immediately, in 3-6 months, 6-12 months, or never?) and what are the barriers (if any) that they face in being able to use them?

- What type of connection did they use for the session (LAN, DSL, cable)? I also want to know how the connection performed and if they had any connection problems.

- Where did they attend the session from (work, home, or both)?

You need to seriously consider what you want to evaluate and why—look at the broader picture of evaluation as identified by the Kirkpatrick model. With the end-of-course happy sheets as Level 1 evaluation, Levels 3 and 4 are increasingly more difficult to measure, but they are definitely worth tracking. So dispense with Level 1 and go for at least Levels 3 and preferably 4.

Assessing your performance

Now we come to an often overlooked subject: a reflective assessment of your own performance. Spend some time thinking objectively about the successes and shortcomings of the session. Write down the technical issues, the timings, the feedback, and your thoughts about your own presentation and facilitation skills. Be open to learning from mistakes.

Think about what you may change, or find a way of doing something differently.

I recommend that you do this for every session you facilitate. Make your content notes as soon as your session has ended and while it is fresh in your mind. Don't put it off—if you do you will forget something that may be important in making the session more effective the next time.

Review what went well and not so well

Be totally honest with yourself—there is no point otherwise. What do you think went well? What didn't work as well as expected? What could you do to improve it for next time? You need to ask yourself these questions about both the content and your performance.

- **The content**. Go back over your Session Plan and make notes where you want to make changes for next time you run the session. Perhaps some changes are needed on your slides; perhaps an exercise needs some more time to complete; perhaps you need to cut some content, or increase the interaction. Continue to make small improvements, and soon your sessions will become really polished. It's rare that there will not be some improvement that can be made, even if it's only a little 'tweak' here and there.

- **Your performance**. We are extremely fortunate that we have a full recording of our sessions to review after the event. Most classroom trainers do not have this facility, so don't waste the opportunity it provides for improvement. Sometime after the session, take some time out to watch the recording, concentrating on your own performance. What went well, what went wrong, how can you improve your performance? Did the session flow well? Did the slides work? Did you handle the questions well? What about the breakout rooms? Do you need to give instructions more clearly? Was your voice clear, conversational and did you speak at the right pace?

The only way you can improve is to look at what you could do better and concentrate on those aspects. By being honest with yourself, and perhaps by asking a colleague to critique your performance as well, you will quickly see improvements. No-one is perfect or ever will be—but we should all aim for continuous improvement in what we do.

Post-session learner support

Just because your session has ended, it should not mean the end of the learning. It's important that you provide your learners with further ways to continue learning about the topic you have been training.

You can make resources available to your learners at any time, and in almost any form. There are now many ways to continue communicating with and supporting your learners as they find opportunities to apply what they learned, and it is important to provide that facility for them.

Here are just some of the ways you can provide post-session support to your learners:

- **VLE/LMS**. One way of doing this is through a VLE (virtual learning environment)/LMS (learning management system)—using facilities such as forums, online chat, and downloadable resources. If you do not have a company LMS, then you could look at the Open Source solution, Moodle—it's simple to set up—and it's free (www.moodle.org).

- **Build a community**. As explained earlier in the chapter, communities of practice are now mainstream. It is important to build up your learning community by using systems set up to provide them at no cost—such as LinkedIn or Facebook. Alternatively, look at setting up your own private groups using systems like Ning, Yammer and Elgg—there are many low-cost services out there. Additionally, you could schedule regular Skype sessions for discussions and general social learning activities.

- **Provide further materials**. You can direct learners to use high-quality supportive learning materials like tutorials, videos, demonstrations, simulations and games that are widely available free of charge on the Internet. You can even produce these materials yourself fairly easily with tools like Captivate, Articulate, and Camtasia Studio—there are numerous others that you can use for minimal cost.

- **Supporting your learners on an extended programme**. If your online sessions are run over a period of weeks, with study assignments in between, you can provide regular touch points. Check in with each learner on a regular basis to ensure they understand the assignments, and check that they are progressing well. Don't bombard them with information though, but provide a repository where they can go to get the help and advice they may need.

Learning is not an event — it's a continuous process

As a learning professional it is your duty to provide learners with further access to learning. So remember, your responsibility does not end when you close your classroom door at the end of the course.

Learning is an exciting, rewarding and continuous journey. I hope that through this book I have helped you along your journey to becoming a first-class, professional Live Online Learning Facilitator.

I sincerely hope that you continue your development and learning about the exciting new world of a live online learning.

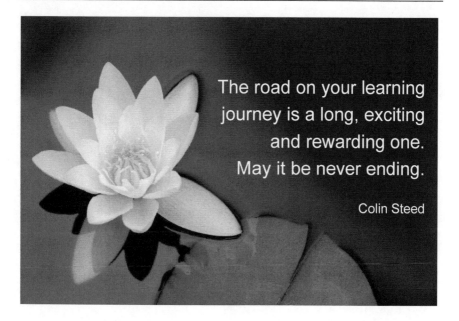

The road on your learning journey is a long, exciting and rewarding one. May it be never ending.

Colin Steed

After reading this book, and practising the skills and techniques that I have covered within its pages, you should have a thorough foundation in facilitating live online learning events—but please do not let it stop there.

Practise as much as you can—read every article, blog and book about the subject that you can find. Collaborate on our Online Learning Facilitator networking site for readers of this book, attend webinars, go to conference sessions, ask for advice and give help on Twitter—basically learn as much as you can about the subject.

And for those of you who are new to web conferencing technology, please do not be daunted by it; all it takes is practice, as with any other software application. Once you get the hang of using it, it becomes second nature and just a tool to enable you to deliver learning events online, with the software in the background.

Enjoy your career in live online learning and please contact me if I can be of any help both now and in the future. I wish you every success.

References & Resources

Here is a list of the references and resources that I have mentioned in the book. With a dynamic nature of the Web, naturally some of the links will go out of date over time, so I have also published these pages on my blog (www.virtualclassroomtrainer.com) so that I can keep it up to date on a regular basis.

Additionally, on the Book Reference Pages of the blog, I will be adding further resources to do with facilitating live online learning sessions, so sign up to receive regular updates.

CHAPTER 1

American Society of Training & Development, State of the Industry Report (2009). http://ow.ly/5Lcqj

Towards Maturity Benchmark (2010). http://ow.ly/5Lcxn

IITT Learning Survey 2011. http://ow.ly/5LcBD

e-Learning Guild Report: Getting Started with Synchronous Training (2010). http://ow.ly/5LcFn

WebEx Training Centre. http://ow.ly/5LcJT

Adobe Connect. http://ow.ly/5LcN9

Microsoft Live Meeting. http://ow.ly/5LcSD

Citrix GoToWebinar. http://ow.ly/5LdTs

Blackboard Collaborate (Elluminate Live!). http://ow.ly/5LdYp

Saba Centra. http://ow.ly/5Le0W

CHAPTER 2

Teaching Today by Geoff Petty. http://ow.ly/5Le2w

Certified Online Learning Facilitator. The IITT. http://ow.ly/5Le5Z

CHAPTER 3

Teaching Today by Geoff Petty. http://ow.ly/5Le2w

George A Miller. http://ow.ly/5Led7

Jeanne Farrington. http://ow.ly/5LegT

John Sweller. http://ow.ly/5LejQ

Richard E Mayer. http://ow.ly/5LenQ; Multimedia Learning by Richard E Mayer. http://ow.ly/5LeuA; e-Learning and the Science of Instruction by Richard E Mayer & Ruth Colvin Clark. http://ow.ly/5LeAx

Cathy Moore, Action Mapping. http://ow.ly/5LeFd

The ADDIE model. http://ow.ly/5LeHx

Gagne's Nine Events of Instruction. http://ow.ly/5LeLu

CHAPTER 4

Visualisation and Instructional Design by John Sweller - http://ow.ly/5LeVL

Brain Rules by Dr John Medina. http://ow.ly/5LeXP

Neil Lasher, The Learning Coach. http://ow.ly/5Lf86

Edmund Arnold – Gutenberg Diagram. http://ow.ly/5Lfil

Garr Reynolds' Blog. http://ow.ly/5LflE

The Presentation Secrets of Steve Jobs: How to Be Insanely Great in Front of Any Audience by Carmine Gallo. http://ow.ly/5LfoE

Presentation Zen: Simple Ideas on Presentation Design and Delivery (Voices That Matter) by Garr Reynolds. http://ow.ly/5LfqU

slide:ology: The Art and Science of Creating Great Presentations: The Art and Science of Presentation Design by Nancy Duarte. http://ow.ly/5Lfzw

Resonate: Present Visual Stories That Transform Audiences by Nancy Duarte. http://ow.ly/5LfCr

Beyond Bullet Points by Cliff Atkinson. http://ow.ly/5LfFF

Better Than Bullet Points by Jane Bozarth. http://ow.ly/5LfHJ

Olivia Mitchell Blog. http://ow.ly/5LfKo

David McCandless, Information is Beautiful. http://ow.ly/5LfOs

Edward Tufte. http://ow.ly/5LfQG

Professor Michael Alley – Assertion/Evidence Model. http://ow.ly/5LfSH

Big Stock Photos. http://ow.ly/5LfWb

iStock Photos. http://ow.ly/5LfZs

British Dyslexia Association. http://ow.ly/5Lg20

Colour Group. http://ow.ly/5Lg9s

CHAPTER 5

SurveyMonkey. http://www.surveymonkey.com

The New Virtual Classroom, Ruth Colvin Clark & Ann Kwinn. http://ow.ly/5Lgid

Moleskine Storyboard Pocket Notebook. http://ow.ly/5Lgln

Colin Steed's blog. http://www.virtualclassroomtrainer.com

CHAPTER 6

Audacity – audio editing software. http://www.audacity.com

Evidence Based Teaching by Geoff Petty. http://ow.ly/5Lhch

1080 Group. http://www.1080group.com/

CHAPTER 7

Performing Rights Society. http://ow.ly/5Lhg6

CHAPTER 8

The New Virtual Classroom, Ruth Colvin Clark & Ann Kwinn. http://ow.ly/5Lhjy

A Cognitive Theory of Multimedia Learning: Implications for Design Principles by Richard E Mayer and Roxana Moreno. http://ow.ly/5LhnH

CHAPTER 9

Elgg. http://www.elgg.org/

Ning. http://www.ning.com/

Yammer. http://www.yammer.com/

Facebook. http://www.facebook.com

LinkedIn. http://www.linkedin.com

Moodle. http://www.moodle.org

Adobe Captivate. http://www.adobe.com/products/captivate.html

Articulate. http://www.articulate.com/

Camtasia Studio. http://www.techsmith.com/

ADDITIONAL RESOURCES – THE BOOKS

As well as the references above, I would like to acknowledge the following books that have helped me form an extensive knowledge of the subject of live online learning.

The New Virtual Classroom by Ruth Colvin Clark & Ann Kwinn. http://ow.ly/5Lhjy

Virtual Training Basics by Cindy Huggett. http://ow.ly/5LinG

Synchronous Trainer's Survival Guide by Jennifer Hoffman. http://ow.ly/5LiRg

E-Learning Guild Report: Getting Started with Synchronous Training (2010) by Patti Shank. http://ow.ly/5LcFn

e-Learning Guild Handbook on Synchronous Training (2007) by Karen Hyder, Ann Kwinn, Ron Miazga, Matthew Murray, Bill Brandon (ed). http://ow.ly/5Ljnk

About the author

Colin Steed has over 35 years experience in the IT training industry. Having spent ten years in the British Airways' IT department, where he was responsible for training computer operations staff, he joined the major IT conference organisers and publishers Infotech in 1978.

He founded Training Information Network and launched the first magazine in the IT training field— *IT Training*—where he edited the publication until it was sold in 1998.

Additionally, he launched *Management Skills & Development* magazine and later in 1995, he was instrumental in founding and setting up the Institute of IT Training, the world's first professional body for IT training professionals.

In 1998, whilst at the Hemmings Group, he co-founded and edited a newly-launched magazine, *IT Skills* and founded the IT Skills Research Programme—providing IT skills and development intelligence for training providers.

His first book was published by Gower Publishing in 1999, *Web-Based Training*, which was the first book to be published on the subject (the forerunner of live online learning) in Europe.

In February 2000, he was presented with the Institute of IT Training's Colin Corder Award for his achievements and services to the IT training industry.

He was appointed as Chief Executive of the Institute of IT Training in October 2000. In 2002 he was published as one of ten people in IT Training magazine's IT Training Hall of Fame.

Following his charity work for the children's charity NSPCC ChildLine, in 2011 he was awarded Patron status of NSPCC ChildLine to recognise his achievement of raising over £200,000 for the charity since he launched the IITT Charity Auction in 2001.

Colin is a prolific writer and publisher and has had numerous articles and white papers published. He is currently expanding his portfolio of books, white papers, videos and webinars on live online learning.

Contact details

Email: colin_steed@btinternet.com

Twitter: @ColinSteed

Blog: www.virtualclassroomtrainer.com

Website: www.colinsteed.com